NATIONS OF THE WORLD

SWEDEN

Robbie Butler

www.raintreepublishers.co.uk
Visit our website to find out more information about Raintree books.

To order:
 Phone 44 (0) 1865 888113
 Send a fax to 44 (0) 1865 314091
 Visit the Raintree bookshop at www.raintreepublishers.co.uk to browse our catalogue and order online.

First published in Great Britain by Raintree, Halley Court, Jordan Hill, Oxford, OX2 8EJ, part of Harcourt Education Ltd.
Raintree is a registered trademark of Harcourt Education Ltd.

Produced for Raintree by the Brown Reference Group plc
Project Editor: Robert Anderson
Designer: Joan Curtis
Cartographers: Colin Woodman and William Le Bihan
Picture Researcher: Brenda Clynch
Editorial Assistant: Roland Ellis
Indexer: Kay Ollerenshaw

Raintree Publishers
Editors: Isabel Thomas and Kate Buckingham

Printed and bound in Singapore.

ISBN 1 844 21478 8
07 06 05 04 03
10 9 8 7 6 5 4 3 2 1

British Library cataloguing in publication data
Butler, Robbie
    Sweden – (Nations of the world)
    1. Human geography – Sweden – Juvenile literature
    2. Sweden – Geography – Juvenile literature
    I.Title
    914.8'5

A full catalogue is available for this book from the British Library.

Acknowledgements
Front cover: Woman in traditional Swedish costume.
Title page: Maypole dancing at midsummer festival.

The acknowledgements on page 128 form part of this copyright page.

Every effort has been made to contact copyright holders of any material reproduced in this book. Any omissions will be rectified in subsequent printings if notice is given to the publishers.

Contents

Foreword

Since ancient times, people have gathered together in communities where they could share and trade resources and strive to build a safe and happy environment. Gradually, as populations grew and societies became more complex, communities expanded to become nations – groups of people who felt sufficiently bound by a common heritage to work together for a shared future.

Land has usually played an important role in defining a nation. People have a natural affection for the landscape in which they grew up. They are proud of its natural beauties – the mountains, rivers and forests – and of the towns and cities that flourish there. People are proud, too, of their nation's history – the shared struggles and achievements that have shaped the way they live today.

Religion, culture, race and lifestyle, too, have sometimes played a role in fostering a nation's identity. Often, though, a nation includes people of different races, beliefs and customs. Many may have come from distant countries, and some want to preserve their traditional lifestyles. Nations have rarely been fixed, unchanging things, either territorially or racially. Throughout history, borders have changed, often under the pressure of war, and people have migrated across the globe in search of a new life or because they are fleeing from oppression or disaster. The world's nations are still changing today: some nations are breaking up and new nations are forming.

Sweden is a small, prosperous country situated on the **Scandinavian Peninsula** and separated from western Europe by the Baltic Sea. Since early times, the Swedes have always looked outwards, sometimes in a spirit of trade and sometimes in a spirit of conquest. The Swedish Vikings, for example, used swift, robust longships to trade with, and sometimes raid, their European neighbours. Today, modern Swedes are debating whether to turn to Europe again. The opening of the Öresund Link, a bridge and tunnel crossing the narrow strait between Sweden and Denmark, may signal an age of European co-operation and unity.

Introduction

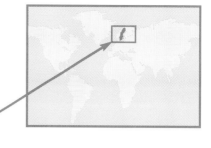

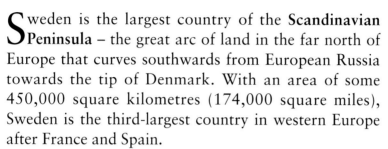

Sweden is the largest country of the **Scandinavian Peninsula** – the great arc of land in the far north of Europe that curves southwards from European Russia towards the tip of Denmark. With an area of some 450,000 square kilometres (174,000 square miles), Sweden is the third-largest country in western Europe after France and Spain.

Sweden is part of Scandinavia – a group of countries in northern Europe that are bound together not only by their shared geography but also by many historical and political ties. To the west lies Norway, with which Sweden was united for nearly a century until 1905. The two countries share one of the longest land borders in the world.

Sweden is even more closely linked with its other Scandinavian neighbour, Finland, which lies to the north and east. Indeed, until 1809, Finland was part of Sweden. The two countries share a land border in the north. In the south, they are divided only by the narrow stretch of the Baltic Sea usually called the Gulf of Bothnia but known to the Swedes as the Inland Sea. Numerous ferries connect the countries, shuttling between the Swedish capital, Stockholm, and Finland's capital, Helsinki.

Sweden's other nearest neighbour is Denmark, from which it is separated by a narrow stretch of water – the Öresund, called the Sound in English. At its narrowest point, the Öresund is only 6 kilometres (3½ miles) wide.

Although most of Sweden's land is covered by forest, there are also rich pasture lands, particularly in the south and centre of the country.

The Swedes are justly proud of their beautiful and varied country, whose wonders include some 100,000 lakes and more than 20,000 islands along the jagged sea coasts. Sweden's rich **natural resources** help account for its present-day prosperity. The national anthem celebrates the 'green meadows' and mountains that make Sweden the 'loveliest land on Earth'.

POLITICS AND GOVERNMENT

The colours of the Swedish flag come from the country's medieval coat of arms.

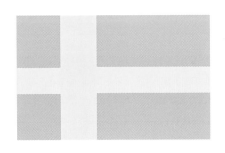

Sweden's full official name is the Kingdom of Sweden. Historically, the nation was ruled by dynasties (families) of kings and queens. Today, the country is a parliamentary democracy, and the king or queen is only the symbolic head of state, with no real power. The Swedes own name for their country is Sverige, a word that derives from the name of one of the ancient peoples who lived in the country.

The Swedish flag – a yellow cross on a blue background – dates back to at least the 17th century, when Swedish ships are first recorded as flying the design. The flag is based on that of Sweden's neighbour Denmark. Every year, Sweden celebrates Flag Day on 6 June.

Sweden also has two **coats of arms**. The Lesser Coat of Arms, the most widely used, has three gold crowns on a blue background. According to legend, the design was used first by King Magnus II Eriksson (1316–74), who adopted the device (sign) to symbolize his title, 'King of Sweden, Norway and Scania'. The Greater Coat of Arms is used by the monarch and

*Sweden's currency is the **krona**. There are 20, 50, 100, 500, 1000 and 10,000-krona notes. Sweden is still uncertain whether or not to join the European single currency. Joining would mean the **krona** would be replaced by the euro.*

POPULATION DENSITY

The vast majority of Swedes live in the central and southern regions of the country, which were the historic homelands of the Swedes. There the climate is mild and the land is fertile.

PERSONS	
Per sq km	Per sq mile
5	13
20	52
100	259
500	1259

sometimes by government. It contains several of the arms (heraldic symbols) of Sweden's dynasties of kings, including the triple crown, the Folkunga Lion and that of the current ruling house.

The country's currency is the *krona*, which divides into 100 *öre*.

People and languages

Sweden has a population of 8.9 million, making an average of only 22 people per square kilometre (57 per square mile). However, large areas of the country are uninhabited. Most people live in the southern part of the country, in or near the three principal cities of Stockholm, Göteborg (Gothenburg) and Malmö.

Until the middle of the 20th century, almost everyone living in Sweden was native-born and there were few other ethnic groups. Swedish was the mother tongue of nearly all the people, and 95 per cent of Swedes belonged to the national church, the **Lutheran Church** of Sweden. Since World War Two (1939–45), however, there has been a

The chart below shows the steady growth of the Swedish population since 1775.

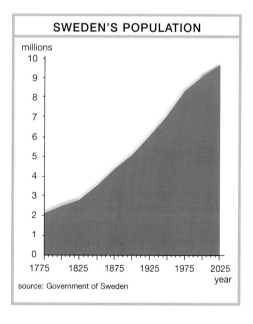

SWEDEN'S POPULATION

millions

source: Government of Sweden

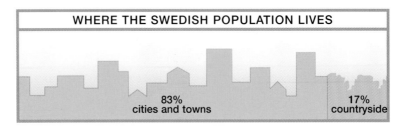

WHERE THE SWEDISH POPULATION LIVES

83%
cities and towns

17%
countryside

Less than one-fifth of Swedes live in the countryside. Most live in the towns and cities of southern Sweden.

Sweden has the fifth oldest population in the world. About 22 per cent of Swedes are older than 65.

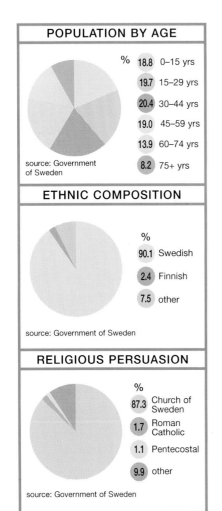

POPULATION BY AGE

%	
18.8	0–15 yrs
19.7	15–29 yrs
20.4	30–44 yrs
19.0	45–59 yrs
13.9	60–74 yrs
8.2	75+ yrs

source: Government of Sweden

ETHNIC COMPOSITION

%	
90.1	Swedish
2.4	Finnish
7.5	other

source: Government of Sweden

RELIGIOUS PERSUASION

%	
87.3	Church of Sweden
1.7	Roman Catholic
1.1	Pentecostal
9.9	other

source: Government of Sweden

good deal of **immigration** to Sweden, and now some 13 per cent of Swedes are either foreign-born or have a parent who was born outside Sweden.

Because there is a common labour market in the Scandinavian countries, most immigrants come from other Scandinavian countries, particularly from Finland. After joining the **European Union** (EU) in 1995, Sweden continued to accept some immigrants and refugees – even though the EU operates a strict immigration policy towards people born outside its area.

There are two minority groups native to Sweden, each of which has its own language. Along the Finnish border in the north-east live about 30,000 Finnish-speaking Swedes. The **Sami** (Lapp) population of Sweden numbers some 17,000. The Sami are scattered across the interior of northern Sweden and live also in the nearby northern areas of Norway, Finland and Russia; there are some 50,000 to 60,000 of them in all. Historically hunters and fishers, they are best known for their reindeer herding. Today, however, few Sami follow the traditional **nomadic** way of life, and most earn a living from fishing, farming or mining.

The majority of Swedes live in towns or cities, working in service or manufacturing jobs. They pay very high taxes, but they enjoy an exceptionally high standard of living. Their **welfare state** – the government-run

The national anthem

Sweden's national anthem, 'Du gamla, du fria', celebrates the mountains and meadows of the nation's landscape. The words were written by the 19th-century folklorist Richard Dybeck and were set to a folk melody from the county of Västmanland. The song proved very popular and was eventually adopted as the national anthem. Here is a translation of the words:

You ancient, you freeborn, you
mountainous North.
In beauty and peace our hearts beguiling,
I greet you, the loveliest land on Earth.
Your sun, your skies, your green meadows
smiling.
Your sun, your skies, your green meadows
smiling.

Your throne rests on memories from great
days of yore,
When worldwide renown was valour's
reward.
I know that to your name you are as true
as before.
O I would live and die in Sweden.
O I would live and die in Sweden.

system that was created after World War Two – has often been held up as a model to the rest of the world.

Sweden's economy ran into trouble in the early 1990s, forcing the government to introduce strict controls on public spending. Today, though, the country is emerging from a difficult period and making a relatively successful transition from an industry-based economy to a service-based one. At the start of the 21st century, Sweden remains one of the richest and most stable countries in Europe – and one of the most envied.

Pronouncing Swedish words

Throughout this book, you may notice that Swedish has some unusual-looking letters – å, ä and ö. This gives the Swedish alphabet 29 letters rather than the 26 found in English. Some of these letters are pronounced as follows:

å   pronounced like *oa* in 'boat'
ä   pronounced like *e* in 'pet'
ö   pronounced like *i* in 'bird'
ej   pronounced like *a* in 'gate'
g   before e, i, y, ä or ö, pronounced like *y* in 'yet'
j   pronounced like *y* in 'yet'
k   before e, i, y, ä or ö, pronounced like *sh* in 'shut'.

Another distinctive feature of spoken Swedish is that it is almost sung. Visitors find this melody of the language difficult to imitate.

Land and cities

'[Stockholm] isn't a city at all … It is simply a rather large village, set in the middle of some forest and some lakes.'

Swedish film director Ingmar Bergman (born 1918)

Sweden's national identity is closely linked to its land. The people are deeply proud and respectful of the rich variety of landscapes their country has to offer – the vast forests of spruce and pine and **glacier**-hewn mountains in the north, the rich fertile plains of the south and the long, rugged coastline.

The close relationship between land and people is hallowed in the *Allemansrätt*, or 'the Right of Common Access' (see page 37), an unwritten law Swedish people hold dear. Swedes believe they have the right to walk anywhere they want to and to spend the night anywhere, as long as they do not damage wildlife or crop land or intrude on others' privacy.

In contrast to southern Sweden, the cold northern wilderness, Norrland (North Land), is only thinly populated. All of Sweden's major cities lie in the south of the country. In the northern half of Sweden, by contrast, there are only two towns with more than 50,000 people.

Sweden's cities are clean and prosperous. They are well planned, with efficient transportation systems and lots of amenities such as hospitals and schools. Many big cities, such as Stockholm and Göteborg, have preserved their historic centres. The cities are small compared to other European cities. Even the largest, Stockholm, has a population of only 685,000 people – slightly larger than that of Glasgow.

Sweden's capital, Stockholm, is built on an archipelago (chain of islands) on the Baltic Sea. Its expanses of water and parkland give it an almost rural feel.

FACT FILE

- Reputedly, Sweden's terrain includes some 100,000 lakes. The largest are lakes Vänern and Vättern.

- The native **Sami** are one of Sweden's most important ethnic minorities. Once widely known as the Lapps, they are today known by their own name for themselves.

- About one-seventh of Sweden's land lies north of the Arctic Circle. This area is sometimes called the 'Land of the Midnight Sun' because, in midsummer, the sun shines here for 24 hours a day.

- Only four Swedish cities have a population of more than 200,000.

TERRAIN

At various times, the whole of **Scandinavia** has been covered by giant ice sheets known as glaciers. During the most recent ice age, which ended about 10,000 years ago, Sweden's landscape was shaped by the movement and weight of the glaciers as they grew and shrank with the changes in temperature. In the country's central region, for example, the ice pressed the landscape flat below sea level, creating an area of plains and lakes.

Land, lakes and rivers

These mountains in Norrland's remote Sarek National Park were given their distinctive shape by the movement of glaciers thousands of years ago.

Traditionally, Sweden is divided into three broad regions – Norrland, Svealand and Götaland. In the far north is Norrland, a land of forests and mountains. In the western part of Norrland are the Kölen Mountains that divide Sweden from Norway. The mountains are part of the great Caledonian range, which extends under the North Sea and into Scotland and Ireland. In the northern part of the range is Sweden's highest mountain, Kebnekaise (Mount Kebne), which rises to 2123 metres (6965 feet).

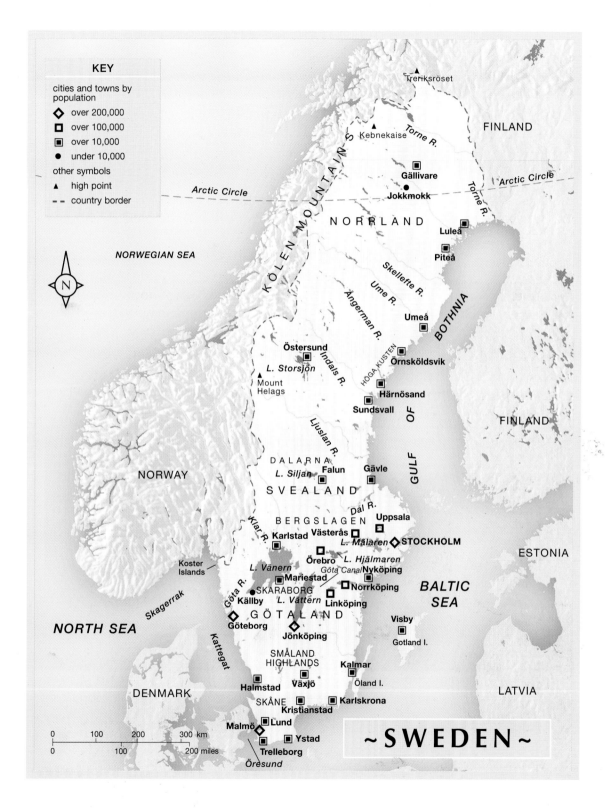

KEY

cities and towns by population

◇ over 200,000
▢ over 100,000
▣ over 10,000
● under 10,000

other symbols

▲ high point
-- country border

NORWEGIAN SEA

Arctic Circle

Treriksröset ▲

FINLAND

Kebnekaise ▲

Torne R.

Arctic Circle

▣ Gällivare

● Jokkmokk

Torne R.

NORRLAND

▣ Luleå

▣ Piteå

GULF OF BOTHNIA

Skellefte R.

Ume R.

Ångerman R.

▣ Umeå

FINLAND

Östersund ▣

Indals R.

HÖGA KUSTEN

▣ Örnsköldsvik

L. Storsjön

▲ Mount Helags

▣ Härnösand

▣ Sundsvall

Ljusian R.

DALARNA

L. Siljan ▣ Falun

▣ Gävle

SVEALAND

Dal R.

BERGSLAGEN ▣ Uppsala

Klar R.

▣ Karlstad Västerås ▣

L. Mälaren ◇ STOCKHOLM

ESTONIA

Örebro ▣ L. Hjälmaren

Koster Islands

Göta R.

L. Vänern

Göta Canal ▣ Nyköping

BALTIC SEA

▣ Mariestad

● SKARABORG

● Källby L. Vättern ▣ Norrköping

▣ Linköping

GÖTALAND

◇ Göteborg

● Jönköping

Visby ▣

Gotland I.

NORTH SEA

SMÅLAND HIGHLANDS

Kalmar ▣

Skagerrak

Kattegat

▣ Växjö

Öland I.

LATVIA

DENMARK

▣ Halmstad

SKÅNE ▣ Kristianstad

▣ Karlskrona

Malmö ◇ ▣ Lund

● Ystad

Trelleborg ▣

Öresund

NORWAY

| 0 | 100 | 200 | 300 km |
| 0 | 100 | 200 miles |

~ **S W E D E N** ~

15

Sweden's longest river is the Torne, in the far northern part of Sweden. It is 570 km (354 miles) long.

The far northern part of Norrland lies north of the Arctic Circle. The landscape there becomes a rugged, treeless marshland known as **tundra**. In summer, the tundra becomes colourful with bilberries and wild strawberries. Throughout Norrland, fast-flowing rivers tumble down from the mountains and into the Gulf of Bothnia.

To the south of Norrland is Svealand – Land of the Svear. The Svear were the ancient inhabitants of this region. The area is much flatter and is a mixture of forest and farmland. It is also home to the country's largest lakes – Vänern and Vättern.

Götaland is Sweden's most southerly region. It gets its name – Land of the Goths – from another ancient people. Northern Götaland resembles Svealand, but towards the south, the landscape rises into hilly woodlands. The poor, stony soils of this region make farming difficult. At Götaland's southerly tip, however, are fertile plains.

SWEDEN'S LANDFORMS

● **Mountains**
The Kölen Mountains mark the boundary between north-west Sweden and north-east Norway. Numerous small glaciers are found in the mountains, the most southern of which lies on Mount Helags. The highest peaks, including Kebnekaise, are in the north of the range. Most of Sweden's rivers have their source in the Kölen Mountains, including one of the longest, the Klar–Göta.

● **Småland Highlands**
This area of rocky, wooded upland lies in the middle of southern Sweden. It is sometimes known as the Götaland Plateau. The area rises to a maximum of about 350 metres (1146 feet) above sea level. The soils are very poor and stony, and few people live in the area.

NORRLAND

SVEALAND

L. Vänern

L. Vättern

GÖTALAND

● **Northern Highlands**
The Northern Highlands stretch from the Kölen Mountains to the Gulf of Bothnia. Numerous swift rivers cut south-east through the land, sometimes opening out into long lakes. Towards the coast, the land is mostly low lying. There the rivers open out into fertile valleys. Most of Norrland's population lives in these valleys or on the coast.

● **Swedish lowland**
This area of lowland plains is made up of rich farmlands and woods, and is home to the country's largest lakes, Vänern and Vättern. It is also Sweden's most densely populated region.

Sweden's soils

Like its landscapes, Sweden's soil types were formed by glacial movement thousands of years ago. As glaciers passed across the land, they ground the rock into a rough layer of soil, known as till. Till is the most common soil type in Sweden. Till formed from granite is poor in nutrients and is most common in the north of Sweden. By contrast, till formed from limestone makes a rich, brown soil and is found in pockets across southern Sweden. In central Sweden, there are rich clayey soils, which originally came from the bottom of the sea. Thousands of years ago, this part of Sweden was lifted up from under the sea.

A spectacular coastline

Sweden's long, ragged coastline faces the North Sea to the south-west and the Baltic Sea to the east. The coastline stretches for 7564 kilometres (4690 miles). Inlets cut deep inland, and hundreds of rounded, wooded islands dot the shoreline. The islands have been worn into their rounded shape by the movement of glaciers during the ice age. These collections of islands, or **archipelagos**, are called *skärgården* in Swedish. Sweden's capital, Stockholm, is in part built on such an archipelago.

At some places, the sea has worn Sweden's coastline into fantastic shapes. At Hovs Hallar, in Skåne in southern Sweden, crashing waves have smashed and worn the red-stone cliff into looming towers. On the island of Öland, the Baltic Sea has weathered the limestone into similar pillars of rock, called *rauker* in Swedish.

These towering limestone pillars (rauker) are found on the coast of Öland, near Högby.

A land of forests

Almost 70 per cent of Sweden is covered by forests. These forests are mostly made up of **coniferous** (cone-bearing) trees – such as Scotch pine and Norwegian spruce – and birch trees. The birch is a deciduous tree, which means that it loses its leaves in autumn. The birch is very hardy and can adapt to even very cool or inhospitable climates. In Sweden's mountains, birch replaces pine and spruce at higher altitudes. In the mostly treeless subarctic and arctic tundra, a scrubby type of birch survives.

In the southern part of Sweden, the natural vegetation is deciduous forest. The deciduous trees here include birch, aspen, linden, ash, maple and elm. The deciduous forests that once covered Sweden's southern coasts have been largely replaced by farmland or by coniferous tree plantations. North of Lake Vänern is a belt of mixed deciduous and coniferous trees.

Along with fir and spruce, birch is the most common type of tree in Sweden. Unlike these other trees, though, birch is deciduous. This birch forest is in the north-west of Sweden – the trees are just turning golden in the autumn.

THE REGIONS OF SWEDEN

Modern Sweden is divided into 21 *län* (counties). Each *län* is headed by a governor appointed by the national government. The 21 counties are further subdivided into 288 **municipalities**, each named after whatever town is at its centre. There were once more than 2600 local governments. In 1952, however, they were merged into larger units to create a more workable system. Recently, too, a few counties were merged to create the current total of 21.

Each municipality is made up of a municipal centre and a surrounding territory. The administrative responsibilities of these municipalities include social welfare (such as unemployment and housing benefits), childcare, education, fire protection and city planning, as well as recreational and cultural events and facilities.

SWEDEN'S *LÄN*

Sweden is divided into 21 units called counties (*län* in Swedish). Each of the *län* is governed by an elected council. Below is a list of the *län*, together with their capitals, which are marked on the map with a dot.

BLEKINGE Karlskrona
DALARNA Falun
GÄVLEBORG Gävle
GOTLAND Visby
HALLAND Halmstad
JÄMTLAND Östersund
JÖNKÖPING Jönköping
KALMAR Kalmar
KRONOBERG Växjö
NORRBOTTEN Luleå
ÖREBRO Örebro
ÖSTERGÖTLAND Linköping
SKÅNE Malmö
SÖDERMANLAND Nyköping
STOCKHOLM Stockholm
UPPSALA Uppsala
VÄRMLAND Karlstad
VÄSTERBOTTEN Umeå
VÄSTERNORRLAND Härnösand
VÄSTMANLAND Västerås
VÄSTRA GÖTALAND Göteborg

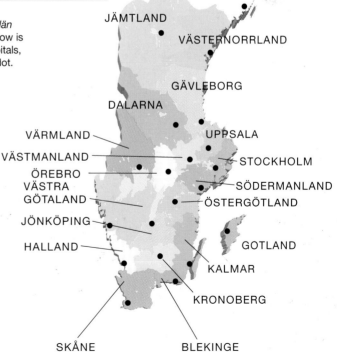

19

Skåne

On the southern tip of Sweden is the old county of Skåne. This is one of the country's most outward-looking regions, partly because of its proximity to Denmark and the rest of Europe just across the narrow Öresund.

In Skåne is a landscape of gently rolling hills and farmlands. There are fields of red poppies and others of yellow rape – a flowering plant prized as a forage crop and as a source of rapeseed oil – together with pasture land. In the *län*'s villages are handsome white churches, while out in the fields are black-painted windmills. Elsewhere, there are dramatic coastlines and large stretches of conifer and beech forest.

Until the 17th century, Skåne was part of Denmark, and the Danes and Swedes were often at war over this fertile territory. Today, the peaceful landscape is dotted with the impressive castles that were built at this time. The flavour of life in Skåne still has a distinctly Danish feel.

The capital of Skåne is the industrial port of Malmö (see pages 48–9). Nearby is the famous medieval city of Lund, with its winding cobbled streets and rose-covered buildings. The city is famous for its university and the streets are busy with students

Ales Stennar

Sweden has many ancient sites that are the remains of monuments built by the Vikings – a group of peoples who once lived throughout Scandinavia (see pages 53–6). One of the most impressive sites is Ales Stennar on the sandy southern coast of Skåne. For centuries, the monument lay buried beneath the sand dunes, but in 1958 the wind blew the sand clear, revealing a stone monument in the shape of a ship. The stone ship is 67 m (220 ft) long and is made up of 56 stones. Two taller monoliths (standing stones) represent the ship's prow and stern. Experts believe that the stone ship marked a Viking meeting place.

rushing to and from lectures on their bicycles. Another important city is Kristianstad (Christian's Town). The city was named in honour of the Danish king Christian IV, who built the town in 1614. It is an elegant city of handsome squares and broad avenues.

Halland and Blekinge

To the north of Skåne is the tiny coastal *län* of Halland. Some parts of its coastline are rocky and others are sandy. Along the sandy stretches are beaches, where people come in summer to sunbathe or windsurf. Old wooden fishing villages alternate with larger towns such as Varberg, with its formidable fortress, and the county capital, Halmstad.

Varberg's museum has a preserved human body from the 14th century – the so-called Bocksten Man.

The county of Blekinge lies to the east of Skåne. The land is hilly and thickly wooded, with a sandy coastline fringed by farmland. The beautiful provincial capital, Karlskrona, stands at the beginning of a windswept archipelago. Karlskrona is named in honour of the Swedish king Charles (Karl) XI (1655–97), who built the city as a home for his Baltic fleet. The city's naval past dominates the modern city. Battleships line the harbour, and the Maritime Museum includes a fine collection of ship figureheads. The largest wooden church in Sweden, the Admiralty Church, looks out over the sea.

Kalmar, Jönköping and Kronoberg

In the thickly forested Småland Highlands are the counties of Kalmar, Jönköping and Kronoberg. The region is famous for its glass industry (see page 86), which was once fuelled by the huge resources of wood also found there. In the mid-19th century, the region was hit by poor harvests. As a result, hundreds of thousands of Swedes emigrated to the USA.

The airy, bright provincial capital of Kalmar stands on a series of offshore islands. The city is dominated by its turreted castle (see page 61), which dates back to medieval times. The castle has a kitchen fireplace big enough to roast three cows at once. Off the coast of Kalmar is the beautiful island of Öland (see box opposite). The modern, high-rise city of Jönköping, in the far north of the region, overlooks the southern shores of Lake Vättern. In the 19th century, the city grew wealthy on the manufacture of matches, which were sold all over the world.

Gotland: the island county

The island county of Gotland is in the Baltic Sea, off the south-east coast of Sweden. The island is famous for its pleasant climate. In the hot summer months, its beaches are packed with tourists.

In the Middle Ages, Gotland's capital, Visby, was a thriving, wealthy port with sixteen churches. Today, the city is much quieter and only one church, the Cathedral of St Mary, is in use. This striking building was built between 1190 and 1225.

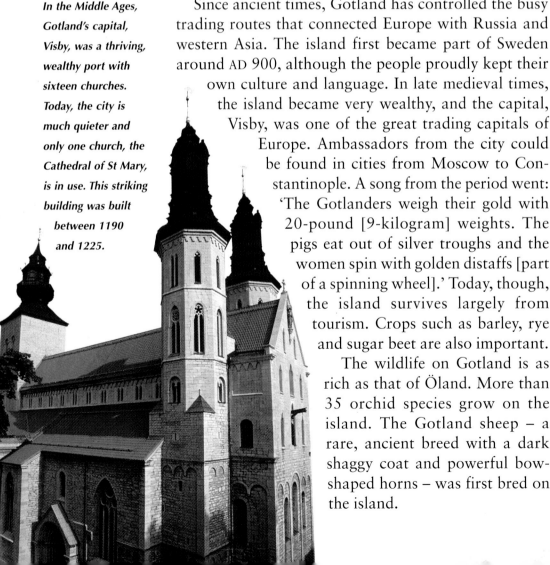

Since ancient times, Gotland has controlled the busy trading routes that connected Europe with Russia and western Asia. The island first became part of Sweden around AD 900, although the people proudly kept their own culture and language. In late medieval times, the island became very wealthy, and the capital, Visby, was one of the great trading capitals of Europe. Ambassadors from the city could be found in cities from Moscow to Constantinople. A song from the period went: 'The Gotlanders weigh their gold with 20-pound [9-kilogram] weights. The pigs eat out of silver troughs and the women spin with golden distaffs [part of a spinning wheel].' Today, though, the island survives largely from tourism. Crops such as barley, rye and sugar beet are also important.

The wildlife on Gotland is as rich as that of Öland. More than 35 orchid species grow on the island. The Gotland sheep – a rare, ancient breed with a dark shaggy coat and powerful bow-shaped horns – was first bred on the island.

Öland

The long, finger-shaped island of Öland is connected to the mainland at Kalmar by a bridge 6 km (4 miles) long. The island is another dramatic creation of the last ice age. In the south, the ice flattened the landscape into a great limestone plain called the Alvaret. In the north, the ice carved out a craggy coastline dominated by spectacular stone pillars called *rauker* (see page 17).

In the 16th and 17th centuries, the Swedish kings often came to hunt here, and the inhabitants were forbidden to own dogs or weapons. The island was vulnerable to attack and many castles were built, though they have long since fallen into ruins. Today, the island is popular with young people, who in summer come here to walk and swim.

The island is very picturesque. There are old wooden cottages, meadows full of flowers and some 400 windmills. The windmills are all national monuments and are carefully preserved (see left). The main town of the island is Borgholm.

Öland is also a haven for plant and wildlife. In the spring and summer, brightly coloured flowers burst from the thin soil of the heathland that covers the Alvaret, including rare species such as the Öland rock rose and blue globe daisy. In the dark, mysterious Trolls Forest are misshapen pine sand oaks.

The land of the Goths

The central region of southern Sweden was the ancient home of the Goths – Götaland. Lake Vättern slices deep into the territory, dividing it in two. Västra Götaland (West Götaland) consists of the old counties of Skaraborg, Älvsborg and Göteborg and Bohus. The eastern part is called Östergötland (East Götaland). The southern section of Sweden's largest lake, Lake Vänern, dominates the landscape of Västra Götaland. The 579-kilometre (360-mile) Göta Canal (see page 91) cuts through the region. It connects the city of Göteborg (see pages 46–7) on the west coast with the Baltic Sea, south of Stockholm.

North of Göteborg, the picturesque coast stretches towards Norway. Holidaymakers flock to the area to visit its tiny fishing villages, unspoiled coves and fjords and hundreds of offshore islands. At Tanumshede (see page 52), some of Sweden's earliest inhabitants carved images of their world into the ice-smoothed rock. Off the northern tip of the county are the rugged Koster Islands, Sweden's most westerly inhabited islands.

Jutting into Lake Vänern is the 17th-century Läckö Castle. The landscape of central and southern Sweden is dotted with many castles and fortresses, bearing witness to the country's troubled past.

Lake Vänern

Between southern and central Sweden are the country's biggest lakes – Vättern and Vänern. At 5584 sq km (2156 sq miles), Lake Vänern is one of the world's largest inland lakes. It is so big that seabirds nest there, including water pipits and turnstones. Commercial fishing is an important industry of the area and accounts for 80% of the catch. Many people, though, come to the lake to fish for pleasure.

Lake Vänern could once boast the most productive salmon waters in Sweden until the construction of **hydroelectric** dams destroyed the spawning grounds. The Vänern salmon became almost extinct by the 1970s. In an attempt to repair the damage, hatcheries raise and release brown trout and salmon into the lake. Stocks of all fish in the lake still remain very low, however.

Between lakes Vänern and Vättern is the wooded area of Skaraborg. The rocky plateau of Kinekulle is the most varied natural site in Sweden, with deciduous woodlands, meadows, pastures and limestone plains devoid of trees. The area is rich in wildflowers, including cowslips, lady's slippers, wild cherry and, in early summer, the strongly fragrant bear garlic. The area's main town, Mariestad, is a quiet, handsome town that overlooks Lake Vänern. Boats cruise out of its harbour on their way to the Göta Canal. Skaraborg is also rich in Viking remains. At Källby, an ancient burial site is marked by two carved stones, one showing the Viking thunder god, Thor.

The county of Östergötland stretches from Lake Vättern to the Baltic. It is a pleasant landscape of fields, canals and rivers. The county capital is Linköping, which stands on the Göta Canal. The town is criss-crossed by canals and is graced with many fine old churches. To the north-east is the industrial city of Norrköping, whose skyline is dominated by old red-brick mills, which once powered the city's textile industry. Today, though, the city is famous for its vibrant youth culture and exciting music scene. The city

The word 'köping', found in many of Sweden's place-names, means 'large community'.

also has many immigrants from Africa and Asia. Many of the city's buildings – and even its bustling trams – are painted a deep mustard yellow.

Stockholm, Uppsala and Södermanland

Together, the counties of Stockholm, Uppsala and Södermanland form the heartland of modern Sweden, home to about one-fifth of the population. The region is dominated by Sweden's beautiful capital, Stockholm (see pages 38–45). The sea beyond the capital is scattered with hundreds of pine-covered islands and islets. In summer, the Stockholm Archipelago, as it is called, makes a striking picture of deep-blue sea dotted with green, and the air is full of the smell of fresh pine. In winter, though, the Baltic often freezes and the inhabitants of the islands can sometimes be stranded.

To the north and west of Stockholm county is the county of Uppsala (Uppland). The county capital is Uppsala, one of Sweden's most ancient cities. It was once the capital of the kingdom of the Svear. Just outside the modern city are the burial mounds of the Svear's ancient pagan kings. Today, Uppsala is famous for its prestigious university, founded in 1477. The sleepy county of Södermanland lies to the south of Stockholm. Its capital, Nyköping, is famous as a centre for textile manufacture.

Boats are moored on the wooded islands of the Stockholm Archipelago. Small ferries criss-cross between the islands carrying goods and passengers. On smaller islands, travellers waiting to be picked up by a ferry have to wave a flag – or at night light a torch – to attract attention.

Central Sweden

To the north of Sweden's great lakes are the four counties of Örebro, Värmland, Västmanland and Dalarna. Together, these form the historic heartlands of Svealand. The region is not densely settled and is made up of forests and farmland, rivers and lakes. In the centre of the region, covering parts of Värmland, Västmanland and Dalarna, is the mountainous Bergslagen region, long an important centre for iron-ore mining.

This picturesque, secluded church stands beside a lake in Gräsmark in Värmland.

Värmland borders Norway and its people even speak Swedish with a slight Norwegian accent. Almost three-quarters of Värmland is spruce and pine forests. The forests, together with the county's deposits of iron ore, provide its inhabitants with much of their income. The county capital is Karlstad, the scene of the treaty ending the union of Sweden and Norway in 1905.

To the east of Värmland is another county of forests and lakes – Örebro. Its bustling capital, which shares its name with the county, is Sweden's sixth-largest city. It stands on the shore of Lake Hjälmaren. In spring, thousands of whooper swans settle on the lake on their way to nesting grounds in the north. Still further east is the county of Västmanland. Its ancient capital, Västerås, overlooks Lake Mälaren. It is an important inland port and is the centre of the Swedish electrical industry.

Further north, the landscape becomes more hilly. This is the picturesque region of Dalarna, with its lush, rolling meadows and villages of red-painted cottages. The heart of Dalarna is Lake Siljan, whose shores are dotted with some of Sweden's prettiest towns and villages.

Many of the place-names of northern Sweden derive from the Sami language: the word 'kaisse', for example, means 'pointed or craggy mountain', 'jokk' means 'stream' and 'lule' means 'eastern'.

The region is famous for its folk crafts, particularly the brightly painted wooden horses known as *dalahästar* (see page 104). In summer, the lakeside is crowded with tourists. Towards the west, the land becomes more mountainous. Dalarna's capital is Falun.

The northern counties

In Norrland are five large counties – Gävleborg, Västernorrland, Jämtland, Västerbotten and Norrbotten. Together, they make up one of Europe's last wildernesses. There are vast, dark forests, spectacular mountains and fast-flowing rivers. Herds of reindeer roam the land, providing some Sami people with their livelihoods (see pages 30–1). Norrland has five of Sweden's national parks. Only the hardiest of walkers attempt to explore their beautiful, wild landscapes.

Only a few more than a million people live in the whole region and there are few towns of any size. The largest is Umeå, the capital of Västerbotten. It has a

The icy Vindelälv River meanders through the wild, remote landscape of Västerbotten.

population of about 95,000. The modern capital of Jämtland, Östersund, overlooks Lake Storsjön and is made up of apartment blocks with quadruple-glazed windows to keep out the winter cold. The lake is said to be inhabited by a dog-headed monster called the *Storsjöodjuret*. In the late 19th century, King Oscar II (1829–1907) tried to catch the monster – but to no avail.

The most northerly town in Sweden – and the last stop on the northern railway – is Gällivare, which lies north of the Arctic Circle. The surrounding area is rich in iron ore and mines scar the landscape. At the very northern tip of Sweden is the Treriksröset, a cairn (rock pile) marking the point where the territories of Sweden, Norway and Finland meet.

In contrast to the inland wilderness, the coastline bordering the Gulf of Bothnia is relatively built up. The northern forests that once reached to the shoreline have been gradually cleared to make way for the region's modern, spacious towns and cities. In the past, when towns were few and far between, people from outlying villages who wanted to go to church had to stay overnight in wooden cottages called *kyrkstäder* (parish villages). One stretch of coast – the Höga Kusten (High Coast) – is famous for its wild beauty (see box).

Most of the best Swedish ski resorts are in Jämtland in the southern part of Norrland. These include Storlien, Duved and Åre, where World Cup skiing events have been held.

The Höga Kusten

The Höga Kusten (High Coast) stretches along Sweden's east coast from the town of Härnösand in the south to Örnköldsvik in the north. This is one of the country's most beautiful areas, made up of sheer cliffs, sandy coves and rugged islands. The Höga Kusten is rich in wildlife – including rare bird species such as the white-backed woodpecker and the coal tit – and hundreds of flower species. Today, it is possible to walk the whole coast by following the 130-km-long (80-mile) Höga Kusten Leden (High Coast Path). Near the beginning of the trail, just north of Härnösand, is a giant suspension bridge crossing the Ångerman River. At 180 m (590 ft) high, the bridge is Sweden's tallest structure. In the north, the path skirts the Skuleskogen National Park.

The Sami and their homelands

The Sami – formerly known as the Lapps – were the earliest native inhabitants of the Scandinavian **Peninsula**. Sami communities can be found in the northernmost areas of Norway, Sweden, Finland and Russia.

Many scholars argue that the Sami are one of the oldest peoples in Europe, who inhabited Scandinavia long before the arrival of the peoples who make up modern Sweden, Norway and Finland. Over the centuries, these new peoples pushed the Sami northwards into their present homeland. Sami call their land Sápmi, but it is more commonly known as Lapland. In more recent times, Sami lands were seized, the people sent away and their sacred places destroyed.

The Sami language, sometimes called Lappish, is related to Finnish. It is a very practical language, with thousands of words to describe the forests, mountains and weather conditions of the Sami's land. There are numerous words to describe snow and ice. '*Sahpah*', for example, means 'powdery snow', '*saevrie*' means 'thick snow that is dangerous to walk on' and '*ruvveske*' refers to the melting water that collects on the top of ice in spring.

While there are a few Sami-language newspapers, books and radio programmes today, most Sami are bilingual, speaking both Swedish and Sami. Many Sami people campaign for the Sami language to be taught more widely in schools and to be used in official publications.

ARCTIC SEA

Kola Peninsula

NORWEGIAN SEA

Arctic Circle

FINLAND

NORWAY

SWEDEN

BALTIC SEA

RUSSIAN FEDERATION

Left: The Sami homelands (shaded green) stretch across northern Scandinavia as well as the Kola Peninsula in the Russian Federation.

Below: The four colours used in the Sami flag are those used in traditional clothing. The circle represents the Sun and the Moon.

Reindeer have traditionally stood at the heart of Sami life (see page 81). For hundreds of years, the Sami have tended their herds of reindeer, taking them into the uplands to calve in spring and bringing them back to the lowland pastures and forests in winter when they have fattened up. The reindeer provided meat not only for the Sami but also for trade with other peoples. In past times, whole Sami communities migrated with the reindeer herds, but today families remain behind in permanent settlements while herders accompany the animals. Herders use helicopters, scooters and walkie-talkies to assist them with their work. Many Sami work in the fishing industry or as farmers; others have become lawyers, teachers and doctors.

The Sami were badly hit in the wake of the Chernobyl nuclear disaster of 1986. Fallout from the damaged nuclear plant in Ukraine (then part of the Soviet Union) contaminated the lichen on which the Sami reindeer feed, and the meat from some 73,000 reindeer had to be destroyed. Reindeer meat became unfit for human consumption, devastating the Sami economy. A current threat to Sami livelihood comes from the mining, forestry and hydroelectric industries, which are destroying reindeer habitats.

Today, like many native peoples, the Sami are fighting for land rights. Since 1993, the Sami have elected representatives to their own parliament. Sami people are very proud of their culture. Traditional clothing (opposite) is worn by modern Sami at festivals and fairs.

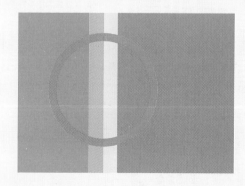

CLIMATE AND WEATHER

Like the rest of Scandinavia, Sweden has a mild climate considering its northern location. Other places with similar latitudes are much colder. Greenland, for instance, has an average temperature that is about 18° C (33° F) colder than Sweden. This is because of the influence of the Gulf Stream, a warm Atlantic current of water that flows northwards from the Equator.

Nevertheless, the weather in Sweden can be very changeable. A few hours of rain can often give way to sun and wind followed by more rainfall.

Sunshine and snow

Sweden's summer is short. The warmest weather occurs between mid-June and mid-August, when most Swedes take their summer holidays. In the south, the winter snows have usually disappeared by late March or early April. However, in the north, there is still likely to be snow in late spring.

Summer is generally not as hot as in most of the rest of northern Europe. In recent years, though, global warming has meant that Stockholm's summer temperatures have been as high as 30° C (86° F). By the end of August, the leaves in the north are starting to turn colour and frost is not uncommon at night. The first snows arrive in the north in September, but the south's longer autumn keeps the snow away until around October.

By November, the snow lies thick on the ground and remains there until March or April. Northernmost Norrland has more than 220 days of snow each year.

RAINFALL AND TEMPERATURE

Despite its northerly location, hundreds of kilometres to the north of Stockholm, the town of Piteå on the Bothnian coast still enjoys a sunny summer. The long, warm days of June and July make it a popular beach resort.

Some coastal parts of the Baltic Sea that are protected by landmasses often freeze in winter and can remain frozen for up to six months.

There is a difference in climate between the eastern and the western parts of the country. Eastern Sweden has stable, dry, sunny weather, with long hot spells in summer and long cold spells in winter. The North Sea washing Sweden's south-west coast brings wet and windy weather.

Night and day

Sweden shares roughly the same latitude as Iceland. Its winter nights and summer days are much longer than in most other countries. In the far north, within the Arctic Circle, there is 24-hour daylight from the end of May to the end of June. April and July are also very bright.

Even as far south as Stockholm, it never gets completely dark in June and there are only a few nightly hours of semi-darkness. From 11 p.m. or midnight, there is a sort of half-light, when the sun is only just below the horizon. This lasts for a few hours, and by 3 a.m. bright daylight has returned.

In winter, daylight is in short supply. Stockholm does not get light until about 9:30 a.m. in December, and it gets dark again at about 3 p.m. In the north (see picture above), there is even more extreme darkness. North of the Arctic Circle, it is dark for 24 hours a day from mid-December to mid-January. In early December and late January, a little light can be seen at high noon.

During these dark months, the aurora borealis, or northern lights – great glowing, shifting shapes of green, blue and orange – illuminate the black sky. In northern Sweden, these haunting lights can be seen about 30 times a year.

WILDLIFE

Animals native to Sweden include wolves, foxes, lemmings, reindeer, bears, elk, lynx, grouse, golden eagles and many other northern birds and mammals. In all, about 60 types of mammals, 230 types of birds, 160 types of fish and 18 types of reptiles, amphibians and related classes of animals are found in the country. Beavers, grey seals and red deer are among the most numerous species, as are reindeer and elk.

Rare animals

Hunting and trapping by humans has almost wiped out Sweden's wolves, but a few still live in the north. Snow-white Arctic foxes (shown above) were once widespread in Sweden, too. At the beginning of the 20th century, though, they had to move north to escape the hunters. Wolverines – powerful weasel-like mammals – are even closer to extinction and were placed under government protection in 1969. There are probably fewer than a hundred left. Though rarely seen, bears still live in the northernmost areas of Sweden. There may be up to 700 bears in Sweden.

North and south

In the northern part of Sweden, large areas of unspoiled wilderness provide habitats for a rich variety of animals and plants. There, ancient spruce, pine and birch forests blanket the lower slopes of the western mountains. The trees here are, on average, 350 years old. Snow buntings, golden eagles, golden plovers and snowy owls haunt the crags and forested slopes. Above the **treeline**, on the open land, wild orchids and other flowers abound.

In southern parts of Sweden, human habitation and farming have destroyed many of the region's natural habitats. Nevertheless, a rich abundance of wildlife can be found, particularly on islands such as Öland. Hundreds of bird species feed and nest along Sweden's lakes, while the thousands of wildflower species are one of the country's national treasures.

Reindeer and elk

The most numerous and best-known Scandinavian animal species is the reindeer. Reindeer in Sweden are not actually wild animals because they are owned by the Sami people. Reindeer can be seen all year round, not just on mountainsides but also in the lowlands. They can pose a serious hazard to traffic, and there are road signs warning of reindeer crossings.

Because the reindeer is so well adapted to the cold conditions, it has spread throughout the Arctic Circle as far as China. Reindeer are herded on a quarter of the Earth's land surface. Reindeer herders often cut distinctive marks into the ears of their animals to denote ownership.

The other animal often associated with Sweden is the elk. There are many thousands of these in the north and also in the forests of Småland. The best time to see them is at dawn and dusk, when they come out to graze at the edge of a clearing. Elk are highly prized by hunters. Since humans continue to drive away their natural predators, the number of elk in Sweden is large, and they are culled every year as well as hunted.

In the water

Sweden's long coasts and many lakes once provided homes for a rich variety of mammals, fish, birds, amphibians and reptiles. Many still exist in these habitats, but environmental pollution has taken its toll. One of the most affected animals is the beautiful Baltic seal.

Fish species found in Swedish waters include cod and mackerel in the salty North Sea, and salmon and pike in the shallower Gulf of Bothnia and in lakes and rivers. The once-common herring and its smaller relation, the Baltic herring, are much rarer and are no longer a staple part of the Swedes' diet (see pages 108–9).

Linnaeus: father of botany

The father of modern botany – the study and classification of plants – was the 18th-century Swede Carl von Linné (1707–78), who is more often known by the name of Linnaeus.

As a boy, Linnaeus showed a deep love of the plants and flowers that grew so abundantly in his native country, gaining him the nickname the 'little botanist'. In 1728, he went to study medicine at the University of Uppsala. There, he spent most of his time studying plants, which were part of the medical curriculum at that time.

In 1735, while in Holland, Linnaeus published a work – the *Systema Naturae* (*System of Nature*) – in which he laid down his ideas about how scientists might impose an order on the abundant forms taken by living things. In 1738, he returned to Sweden and later became a professor at his old university.

As more plant and animal specimens were sent to him from every corner of the globe, Linnaeus's book grew from a slim pamphlet to a multivolume work. He still found time to practise medicine,

though, becoming a physician to the Swedish royal family. Linnaeus also explored the far north of Sweden. On the left he is shown wearing the traditional clothes of the Sami people.

Before Linnaeus, species were named in a haphazard way, with inconsistent, long Latin names. This confusion greatly hampered advances in biology, since one scientist reading the work of another could not always be sure which plants were being referred to.

Linnaeus's idea was to use one Latin name to indicate the genus and one for the species. For instance, Linnaeus named the briar rose the *Rosa canina*. In this name, *Rosa* is the plant's genus (part of the rose family) while *canina* (from the Latin for 'dog') is the species. This binomial (two-name) system rapidly became the standard system for naming not only plant but also animal species. The oldest plant names accepted as valid today are those published in Linnaeus's *Species Plantarum* in 1753. The oldest animal names are those in the tenth edition of *Systema Naturae* (1758).

NATIONAL PARKS

Swedes have always had a deep respect for their country's natural beauty. The unwritten tradition known as *Allemansrätt* affirms every person's right to have the opportunity to commune with nature, to walk anywhere and to spend a night anywhere – as long as he or she does not invade the privacy of home owners or damage crops.

In 1910, Sweden became the first European country to establish national parks – areas of special natural beauty and value that the government holds in trust for the whole nation. Today, there are 26 national parks in Sweden, covering some 20,000 square kilometres (7700 square miles).

The three largest national parks – Stora Sjöfallet, Sarek and Padjelanta – are all in the far northern part of the country. Together, these parks cover some 5520 square kilometres (2132 square miles) of territory. Padjelanta is the biggest national park in Europe and lies almost entirely above the treeline. Its name means 'lighter land' in the Sami language.

In the central region is the Tiveden National Park, a forest area lying about 50 kilometres (30 miles) north of Lake Vättern. Many old, dead trees in this forest are home to a rich variety of rare animals and birds. On the coastal hills of Skåne in the extreme south is the Stenshuvuds National Park, whose forested hillsides support animals not seen elsewhere in Sweden – tree frogs, sand lizards and dormice.

Nordens Ark on the west coast is not a national park but is important as a breeding park for endangered species from Sweden and around the world. The animals there include wolves and Himalayan snow leopards.

NATIONAL PARKS

Sweden's network of national parks ensures that areas of wilderness are preserved in their natural state for future generations. In addition to the parks, there are a large number of nature reserves and other protected areas.

STOCKHOLM: THE CAPITAL ON WATER

Sweden's capital is built on fourteen islands on the country's Baltic shoreline, where Lake Mälaren meets the Saltsjön (Salt Bay). The Swedish novelist Selma Lagerlöf (see page 101) called Stockholm 'the city that floats on water'. Bridges span the narrow bays and channels between the islands. Everywhere there is an abundance of parks, squares and airy green spaces. One-third of the city area is water, while another third is open park and woodland. Elegant old buildings of red stone line the cobblestoned waterfronts, while glass and concrete office buildings dominate the modern, bustling city centre.

The city is Sweden's most important industrial and financial centre, and it is the national capital as well as the home of the country's kings and queens. The city also has a lively arts scene. There are more than 80 museums. In 1998, Stockholm was chosen as the cultural

Yachts dot Stockholm's Saltsjön, the island-strewn bay that links the Baltic Sea with Lake Mälaren. Stockholm is built on fourteen islands that are connected by more than 50 bridges.

STOCKHOLM CITY CENTRE

Stockholm is built on a collection of islands where the Saltsjön – a salty inlet of the Baltic Sea – meets the freshwater Lake Malären. The city is made up of streets (*gatan*) and avenues (*vägen*). Bridges (*bron*) connect the islands (*holmen*).

N

DJURGÅRDEN

Djurgårdsbrunnsviken

Biology Museum

Nordic Museum

Vasa Museum

History Museum

NARVAVAGEN

ÖSTERMALM

STRANDVÄGEN

RIDDARGATAN

LINNEGATAN

STORGATAN

SKEPPARGATAN

Armé Museum

Music Museum

Royal Dramatic Theatre

NYBROGATAN

National Museum

Museum of Modern Art

East Asian Museum

SKEPPSHOLMEN

SKEPPSHOLMBRON

SALTSJÖN

TEATERGATAN

Strömmen

BIRGER JARLSGATAN

BRUNNSGATAN

KUNGSGATAN

JAKOBSBERGSGATAN

MASTER SAMUELSGATAN

HAMNGATAN

Opera House

STRÖMGATAN

NORRMALM

Kulturhuset (House of Culture)

SVEAVÄGEN

Concert House

OLOF PALMESGATAN

DROTTNINGGATAN

KLARABERGSGATAN

VASAGATAN

Central Station

Stadshuset (City Hall)

LAKE MÄLAREN

RIDDARHOLMEN

Riddarholms Kyrkan

GAMLA STAN

STORTORGET

STADSHOLMEN

Tyska Kyrkan

SKEPPSBRON

Börsen

Kungliga Slottet (Royal Palace)

Storkyrkan (Cathedral)

HELGEANDS -HOLMEN

Riksdagshuset (Parliament Building)

VASABRON

Stockholm's history begins at the Gamla Stan, the city's medieval Old Town. Visible here is the church of Tyska Kyrkan, first used by German merchants.

capital of Europe by the **European Union** (EU). Another attraction is the range of restaurants – few other European capitals have more places to eat in relation to the size of their population.

Stockholm's streets are clean and safe and there is little air pollution. Most residents live in high-rise suburbs that spread out to the forests, lakes and meadows around the city. The metropolitan area is served by an efficient system of roads and railways and an underground rail system – the *T-banan* – that has one of the best safety records in the world. Many of the city buses run on ethanol, a grain-based fuel that produces less pollution. Buses and trains are relatively uncrowded compared to those in many of the world's capital cities.

Stockholm's history

No one is quite sure when Stockholm was first founded. The first people to settle in the area were German merchants from the Baltic port of Lübeck, who built a trading post on the small island today known as Stadsholmen (City Island). In the 13th century, Birger Jarl, who was Sweden's regent (a person who governs instead of the monarch), fortified the island and built a high tower topped by the royal symbol – three golden crowns. Today's Royal Palace stands on the site.

As time passed, the town grew busy with trade. Merchants thronged the main square, the Stortorget, and copper-clad church spires rose above the ramshackle warehouses.

Gamla Stan

Stockholm's Gamla Stan (Old Town) occupies the island of Stadsholmen and two smaller islands, Riddarholmen and Helgeandsholmen. Tourists come from all over the world to see the impressive churches and buildings. In medieval times, the centre of Gamla Stan was popular with merchants, whose tall, dark houses can be identified by the grand doorways and coats of arms above them. There are different sorts of merchants in Gamla Stan today, with many antique shops, art galleries and fashionable restaurants.

This bronze copy of the wooden statue of Saint George and the Dragon in the cathedral stands in one of the city's many public squares, the Köpmantorget, in Gamla Stan.

The old city square, the Stortorget, was the centre of the old city and is a good place to begin a tour. On one side of the square is the Börsen, the old stock exchange building, where the modern stock exchange still uses the ground floor. On the floor above is the weekly meeting place for the Swedish Academy, which elects the winners of the **Nobel Prize** for Literature.

Nearby is the Storkyrkan – the cathedral – the site of royal coronations until 1907, when formal coronation ceremonies were rejected by King Gustav V. This is the oldest building in Gamla Stan – part of it dates back to the 12th century. The cathedral's most famous statue is a wooden sculpture of *Saint George and the Dragon*, which was carved in 1489. It is the largest medieval monument in Scandinavia.

Beside the cathedral is the Kungliga Slottet (Royal Palace). It has 608 rooms, some of which are open to visitors. The oldest surviving room interiors date back to the early 17th century. The palace is known for its tapestries. Also to be seen there are the crown jewels and, at noon each day in summer, the changing of the royal guard in the palace yard.

Under the Riksdag

Beneath Stockholm's Gamla Stan lies a rich record of its medieval past. While digging up the Riksdag terrace to make a car park, builders found part of a wall dating from 1530, the cellars of an apothecary's (chemist's) shop and many layers of ruins and objects from later periods. Instead of building a car park, the government decided to set up a museum to celebrate the city's medieval past. The underground Medeltidsmuseum (Medieval Museum) contains models, pictures, boats, skeletons and displays relating to the period. Swedes leave the museum with a sense of how their ancestors lived in the thriving trading city.

Few people live on Riddarholmen (Knight's Island), and there are no restaurants or shops. Before and after work hours, the island is virtually silent. In the bright-red Riddarholm church lie the bodies of almost all of Sweden's royalty. The Swedes have buried their monarchs in this church since 1290.

The third and smallest of the islands of Gamla Stan is Helgeandsholmen (Holy Spirit Island). The island is dominated by the Riksdag (parliament) and the old Riksbank (national bank). Parts of the Riksdag building are open to the public, and visitors can watch politicians debating the issues of the day.

Södermalm and Norrmalm

South of Gamla Stan is the island known as Södermalm, an area of art galleries, restaurants and nightclubs. Locals sometimes call it 'Söder' for short. Traditionally, this was the working-class area of Stockholm. Today, though, the streets bustle with young people.

The financial and business heart of the city lies to the north of Gamla Stan in Norrmalm. It is also an area of modern shopping centres and big department stores. The Hötorget is today an outdoor fruit and vegetable market, but it was once a hay market. The nearby Kulturhuset (House of Culture) holds exhibitions for adults and children.

Norrmalm is also the site of the central station and the central park, Kungsträdgården. The garden once grew fruit and vegetables for the kitchens of the royal

Stockholm may have been named for the drying frames (*stock*) that were set out on the main island (*holm*) in medieval times.

palace. Today, it is one of Stockholm's smallest parks. It includes a winter ice-skating rink, and festivals and special events are held there throughout the year.

On the edge of Norrmalm, above a grocer's shop, is a small museum devoted to Sweden's most famous author, August Strindberg (see page 101) – the Strindbergsmuseet Blå Tornet (Strindberg Museum Blue Tower). The house was Strindberg's home from 1908 until his death in 1912. Inside are many of his personal belongings, including his pen.

Kungsholmen and Östermalm

To the west of Norrmalm lies the island of Kungsholmen, where the ornate Stadshuset (City Hall) and most of the city government buildings can be found. The architect Ragnar Östberg (1866–1945) completed the Stadshuset in 1923. It houses the city council offices and the enormous Blå Hallen (Blue Hall), where Stockholm's most important event, the Nobel Prize dinner, is held each year. The top of the 137-metre-high

Behind the plain brick exterior of Stockholm's City Hall (Stadshuset) is a series of richly decorated rooms and halls, including the Blue Hall and the Golden Hall (below).

(450-foot) tower offers views of the city and beyond. Below the Stadshuset, overlooking Lake Mälaren, are beautiful grass terraces leading down to the bay.

East of Norrmalm is the elegant old residential district of Östermalm. The gilded statues of the Kungliga Dramatiska Teatern (Royal Dramatic Theatre) keep watch over the city harbour. In the same area is the History Museum, which is devoted to the Vikings.

The *T-banan*

Building on Stockholm's underground rail system, the *T-banan,* began in the late 1940s. While the designers of other undergrounds in the world covered the walls in tiles, in Stockholm they decided to decorate their system with the work of more than 70 artists. Paintings adorn not only the ceilings and platforms of the stations but also the tunnel walls along the tracks. The track walls have been transformed into forests, lily ponds and gardens or covered with geometric designs. Of the 99 stations, half have paintings, sculptures or mosaics.

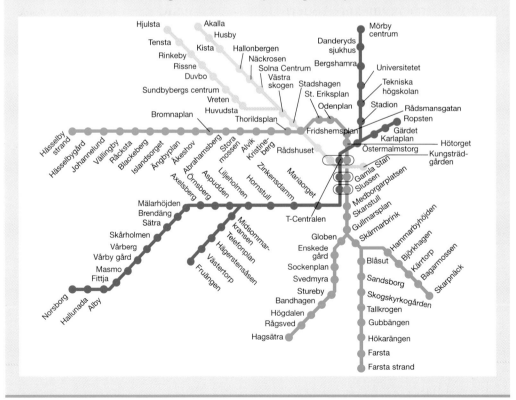

Djurgården

Between Östermalm and Södermalm is the island of Djurgården. The island's lovely parks and museums recall the time when it was a royal game preserve. Also on Djurgården is the 17th-century warship *Vasa*, which was rescued and preserved after sinking in Stockholm harbour. The island is especially popular with children, mostly because of the Junibacken. This is a fairy-tale house where visitors may explore the story-book world of Astrid Lindgren, the children's author who created Pippi Longstocking (see pages 101–2).

One of the most-visited sights outside Stockholm is the Drottningholm Palace. This grandiose 17th-century palace, designed by Tessin the Elder and his son, is today the main home of the Swedish royal family.

Skeppsholmen

The island of Skeppsholmen is famous for its art collections. The Moderna Museet (Museum of Modern Art) houses the work of some famous artists such as Henri Matisse and Pablo Picasso. The Östasiatiska Museet (East Asian Museum) has an impressive collection of Chinese and Japanese antiquities. Just across the footbridge from Skeppsholmen, the National Museet (National Museum) has a collection of Old Master paintings.

GÖTEBORG CITY CENTRE

Maritime Centre

Opera House

Göta River

Rådhus (City Hall)

Stadsmuseet (City Museum)

HAMNGATAN

HAMNGATAN

ÖSTRA HAMNGATAN

VÄSTRA HAMNGATAN

NORRA Hamn Canal SÖDRA

Domkyrkan (Cathedral)

Trädgards-föreningen

STEN STUREGATAN

Kungsparken

N

VASAGATAN

Röhsske Museum

ENGELBREKSGATAN

SÖDRA VÄGEN

SKÅNEGATAN

Museum of Theatre History

Theatre

Concert House

Art Museum

GÖTAPLATSEN

Göteborg's city centre lies to the south of the Göta River. In the old town, closest to the river and harbour, canals zigzag among the narrow streets. To the south of the Hamn Canal is a modern area of parks and broad streets dominated by the large Götaplatsen square. In the square is a giant statue of Poseidon, the ancient Greek god of the sea.

OTHER CITIES

Two other cities compete with Stockholm as Sweden's foremost city – Göteborg and Malmö, both of which are situated on the country's west coast. Both cities are important industrial and administrative centres. At times, they have outshone the capital with their thriving economies and lively streets.

Göteborg

Also known as Gothen-burg, Göteborg lies on Sweden's west coast on the mouth of the Göta River. This bustling, friendly place rivals the capital, Stockholm, as Sweden's leading city. For one thing, it is Scandinavia's largest port, with some 11,000 ships using the harbour every year. Within a ten-minute stroll from the harbour is central Göteborg, with almost 500,000 inhabitants. The whole of Göteborg, including its suburbs, has a population of around 700,000.

Göteborg is built around a network of canals, so that it is sometimes compared to Amsterdam in the Netherlands. The similarity is not surprising considering

A city of superlatives

The inhabitants of Göteborg like to boast of their city's achievements. One of these is the building of the Älvsborgsbron bridge that spans the Göta River. At 918 m (3060 ft) long, it is the longest suspension bridge in Sweden. Under the same river runs the Gnistäng Tunnel, the world's widest motor vehicle tunnel cut through rock. It measures 19 m (62 ft) wide and 712 m (2330 ft) long. What is more, the city is home to three of Sweden's largest companies, including the world-famous car manufacturer Volvo. An annual sporting event is the Gothia Cup, the world's largest football competition, with 28,000 young players from 53 countries taking part.

Many of Göteborg's trams are from the beginning of the 20th century and are resplendent with polished wood, leather seats and gleaming etched glass.

the city's history. In 1621, King Gustavus II Adolph (1594–1632) brought in Dutch engineers to build the city. The clay terrain of the planned site was very unstable, and the engineers wisely advised that no structure should be more than two or three storeys tall. They laid the city out as a moated fortress surrounded by a network of canals.

The best way to see the city is to take a ride on one of the old-fashioned trams that clunk noisily up and down the city streets. There is lots for the visitor to do and enjoy. One of the most popular sights is the Stadsmuseet (City Museum), which contains exhibits focusing on Göteborg's maritime and trading history. One exhibit commemorates a famous sailing ship, the *Göteborg*, which sank in the city harbour in 1745, together with its crew and cargo of Chinese silks and porcelain.

Malmö: close to Europe

Malmö is Sweden's third-largest city and has a population of some 255,000. The city stands on the sandy coast of southern Sweden, overlooking the narrow stretch of water called the Öresund that separates Sweden from Denmark. The Danish capital, Copenhagen, lies just a few kilometres away. Malmö was originally named Malmhaug, which means 'pile of sand'.

MALMÖ CITY CENTRE

St Petri Kyrkan (St Peter's)

Rådhuset (City Hall)

ADELGATAN

STORTORGET

SODARGATAN

MALMÖHUSVÄGEN

Malmöhus

LILLA TORG

BATZARSGATAN

SLOTTSGATAN

HOSPITALGATAN

Technical and Maritime Museum

N

GRYNBODGATAN

Canal

Kungsparken

STORA NYGATAN

Slottsparken

Library

KUNG OSKARS VAG

The medieval city centre of Malmö is made up of old cobbled streets, handsome city squares and green parkland. Outside the historic centre, Malmö is mainly industrial.

Like Göteborg, Malmö owes its past glory to the sea. In medieval times, the city grew prosperous on herrings, which were fished from the nearby waters. For a long time, Malmö was part of Denmark, but in 1658 King Charles X regained the city for Sweden. Soon afterwards, though, the city lost its prosperity and people moved away. By the 18th century, only about 200 people lived there.

Since then, however, the city has recovered. A new harbour was built and the city once again has become a busy port. Today, ships carry Swedish grain, sugar and cement all over the world from the port. The docks are also busy with shipbuilding. The recent opening of the Öresund Link (see page 93), a bridge and tunnel between

Malmö and Copenhagen, should also stimulate the city's prosperity because it will link the city more closely to the European mainland.

The old historic centre of Malmö is surrounded by a system of canals crossed by bridges. At the heart of the city is the Stortorget – a vast cobbled square with a statue of Charles X Gustav on horseback. Overlooking the square are two of the city's finest buildings – the 16th-century Rådhuset (City Hall), which looks like a French château, and the majestic church of St Peter, which was built in the 14th century.

Nearby, is the lively Lilla Torg (Little Square), which has many beautifully restored houses from the 16th century. On summer nights, the inhabitants of Malmö go to the square to stroll and to eat in the cafés there.

Central Malmö has three beautiful parks: Kungsparken, Slottsparken and Pildammsparken. Pildammsparken is the largest landscaped park in Sweden and has a huge amphitheatre. In summer, there are open-air performances of music and dance. Within walking distance, too, is Ribersborg beach, where people often relax when the sun is shining.

On the northern edge of Kungsparken and Slottsparken is Malmöhus, once a mighty Danish castle that guarded the Öresund. For many years, it was used as a prison and later as a place to store grain. The husband of Mary Queen of Scots (1542–87), James Bothwell, was one of its best-known inmates. Today, the castle is home to several museums. There are even more museums nearby in a park that borders the sea.

A multicultural city

Malmö is one of Sweden's most multi-ethnic cities, home to many immigrants from eastern Europe, Latin America, the Middle East and Africa. More than one-fifth of the population is of foreign descent. In the district around the Möllevångstorget square lives a lively mix of nationalities. Every year in August, people of all nationalities gather to celebrate the Malmö Festival. The week-long festivities begin with an enormous traditional Swedish lobster party and go on to include dancing, poetry reading and theatre performances from all over the world.

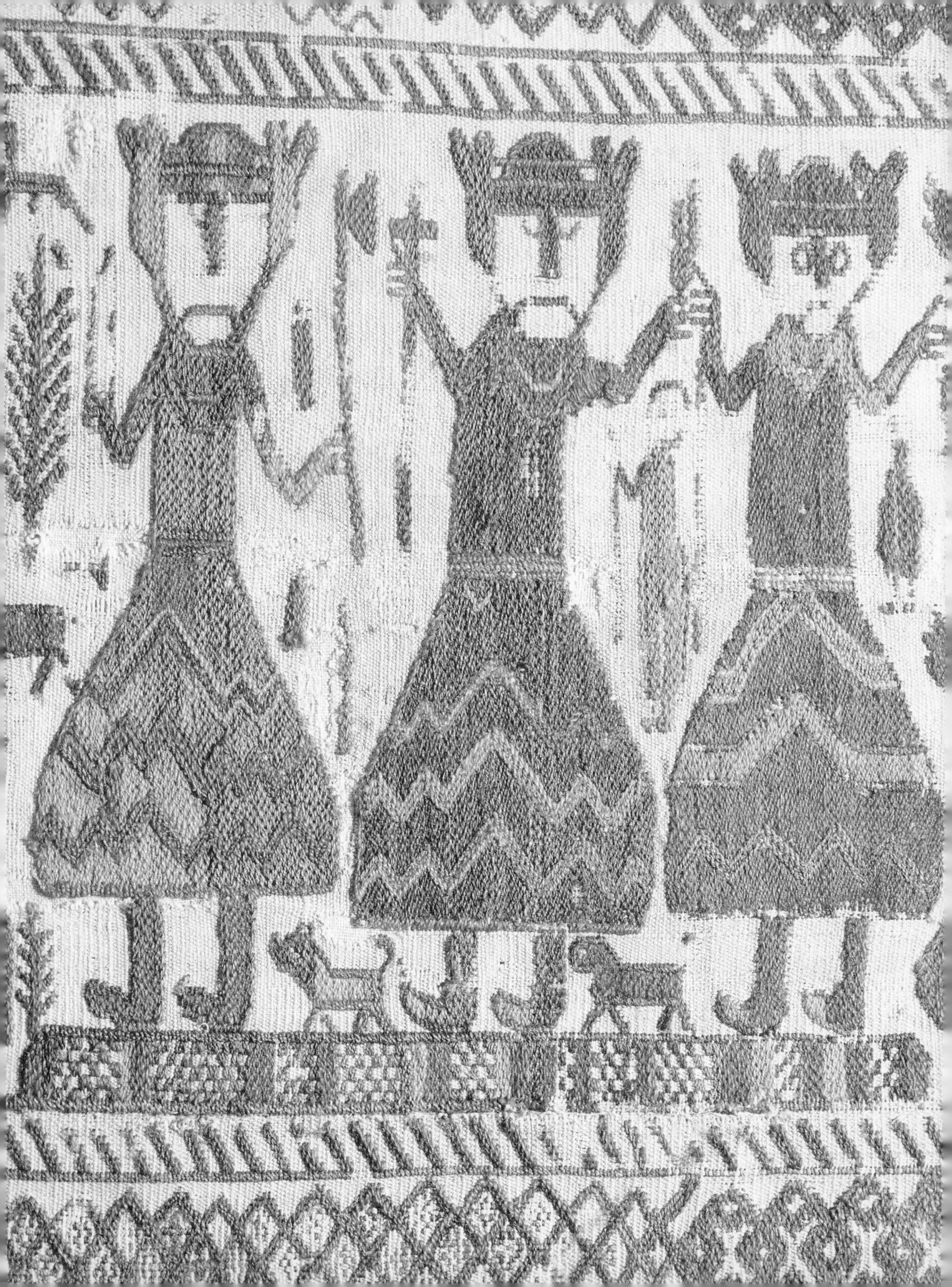

Past and present

'Deliver us, O Lord, from the fury of the Norsemen!'

English prayer of the 8th century AD

Since early times, the Swedes were one of the world's great seafaring people. Despite the relative isolation of their country on the northern fringes of Europe, this meant that they were sometimes able to exert an influence far beyond the confines of their homelands in southern **Scandinavia**. During the Viking age of the 9th to 11th centuries, the Swedish people explored and settled lands across Europe. They were admired as traders and feared as warriors and pillagers.

In the 16th and 17th centuries, a succession of warrior kings built up a great empire, encompassing much of Scandinavia and other lands on the shores of the Baltic Sea. During this time, Sweden became a great European power, intervening in the wars and conflicts that shook the continent. Without the **natural resources** to sustain its empire, though, Sweden failed to become a world power like the United Kingdom or France.

In the 19th century, Sweden turned inwards and looked to its own affairs. Internationally, it adopted a policy of neutrality; it took part in neither of the 20th-century world wars. At home, Swedish governments concentrated on making Sweden a prosperous, safe and tolerant place in which to live. In 1995, Sweden joined the **European Union** (EU). Today, Swedes face the question of whether they should once again turn outwards to Europe, this time in a spirit of co-operation and unity.

This Viking wall hanging shows the three most important Norse gods. On the left is the one-eyed Odin, in the centre is Thor and on the right is Freyr.

FACT FILE

● The term 'Norse' is often applied to the language and culture of the Viking Scandinavians. It comes from a word meaning 'northern'.

● Long before it became a symbol of the German Nazi Party, the swastika – a cross with its arms broken at right angles – was a Norse symbol of fertility and good luck.

● In this book, the kings and queens of Sweden are called by the English version of their names rather than the original Swedish – for example, Charles rather than Karl, and Christina rather than Kristina.

Before history

Rich archaeological evidence allows historians to recreate a picture of Scandinavian life in early times before written records. This time is known as prehistory (before history).

Scattered across the Swedish landscape are large earth mounds called barrows (see page 96), where early peoples buried their dead. The barrows have preserved a rich treasure of goods, ranging from daggers and bronze jewellery to musical instruments and woven woollen garments.

Watery bogs have preserved other remnants of Sweden's early peoples. Wooden ploughs show that they lived by planting crops. From ancient pollen, experts have determined that they grew mainly wheat, barley and millet. Ancient rock carvings, such as those found at Tanumshede in Bohus (right), celebrate the importance of the boats that enabled Scandinavian trade to flourish.

EARLY TIMES

Some 14,000 years ago, thick ice covered the whole of Scandinavia. As the climate grew gradually warmer and the ice melted, human beings migrated across the Baltic Sea and settled in what is today southern Sweden. By 8000–6000 BC, these hunting and fishing people, who used simple stone tools, were living all over the country.

Goths and Svears

Since earliest times, Sweden's inhabitants used the sea, rivers and lakes to move from place to place. By 1500 BC, they had become excellent sailors, extending their trade routes as far as the Danube River hundreds of kilometres to the south. Later still, they traded precious amber and furs with the Roman empire.

During this time, agriculture developed and the population and society became more settled. The people of southern Sweden were called the Goths. Those who lived in the centre of the country were called the Svear (Swedes). In the 1st century

AD, the Roman historian Tacitus, who visited northern Europe, made the first written record of these northern tribes. He described a warrior people with fleets of warships. The Svear gradually came to dominate much of the country. The Swedes' name for their country, Sverige, means 'Land of the Svears'.

The Vikings

Starting in the 9th century, peoples from southern Scandinavia, including Sweden, Norway and Denmark, began to expand into other parts of Europe. These people were called Vikings and spoke a language known as Norse. The Vikings got their name from a Norse word meaning 'bay'.

The Vikings were skilled sailors. They built sturdy, seagoing ships, known as longships (see page 55), which they used to sail throughout the Baltic and North seas and along rivers that took them deep inland. There is evidence that the Vikings were the first Europeans to reach the Americas. Viking sagas (epic stories) record how, in about 1000, Leif Eriksson sailed west from Greenland to a fertile land he called Markland. This was almost certainly the eastern coast of present-day Canada.

The Vikings exploited their naval supremacy to build up trade and to raid and conquer other lands. The Swedish Vikings forged busy trade networks with mighty powers such as the Byzantine empire. They also launched violent raids on coastal communities that were too weak to defend themselves. In other places, they settled and formed new territories. Iceland, Greenland, Normandy, Russia and Sicily were all once Viking lands.

The Vikings

During the 9th and 10th centuries, the Vikings used their longships to trade, raid and settle across Europe and beyond. While the Danes and Norwegians looked for lands to conquer, the Swedes were mostly interested in trade. Objects found in Sweden help scholars identify some of the goods the Vikings coveted – furs and wax from Russia (Rus'), and silks, spices and gems from Constantinople.

At home, the Vikings were good farmers and iron-smiths. They lived in large, shared dwellings known as longhouses (see page 97). The family was at the heart of Viking life. Should a member of a family commit a crime, for example, then every member of the victim's family, including uncles and nephews, had the right to seek vengeance from any member of the criminal's family. In this way, feuds between families might carry on for generations, at great cost in bloodshed to both sides.

Viking law was decided by an assembly called a *thing*. Every community and province had its own *thing*. The local *thing* brought together all freemen to vote. The provincial *thing* comprised elected local representatives and chiefs. The *thing* acted as a court, made the laws and elected chiefs and kings, who could not override the will of the *thing*. The Viking notion

The Norse myths

The Vikings were pagans who believed in many gods. The stories (myths) they told about the gods were eventually recorded in medieval times in long poems called Eddas. According to the Eddas, the gods, ruled by Odin, lived in Asgard and humans lived in Midgard. Both worlds were constantly threatened by giants who lived in the snowy wastes. One day, the Vikings believed, the forces of evil and chaos would overwhelm the gods, and the universe would end in a catastrophe of ice and fire.

The most popular god was Thor (left). The god of thunder, he was a warrior who used a hammer to protect the universe. Odin was the god of death, wisdom and magic. Njord was the god of the sea and his children, Freyr and Freya, were the god of fertility and the goddess of love, respectively. Balder was the most kindly of the gods, but he was killed as a result of scheming by the trickster god, Loki.

Vikings held warriors in high esteem and this is reflected in their myths. They believed that men who died in battle were taken by maidens called Valkyries to Valhalla, a hall where they spent eternity feasting with their fellow warriors.

Viking longships

In the 9th century and later, the appearance on the horizon of low-hulled, square-sailed vessels struck fear into the coastal communities along the Baltic and North seas. These awe-inspiring boats were the longships of the Vikings, as likely coming to plunder as to trade.

The ancient peoples of Scandinavia had long built boats. Rock carvings (see page 52) depict open boats without a keel or sails. While such boats could have navigated rivers or shallow waters close to the shoreline, they were useless on the open sea.

Over centuries of seafaring, however, the Scandinavians perfected the craft of boat building. The Viking longship was first developed in the 7th century, when a keel, which helped stabilize the boat, and a square sail were added to the vessel. The sail was made out of a double thickness of woollen cloth and was often coloured red to attract attention and inspire awe.

The ships were built of oak planks, overlapped like tiles and riveted to a basic framework. They were double ended, often with carved dragon heads

The woollen **sail** could be as large as 100 sq m (1075 sq ft). Its red stripes drew attention to the approach of the ship.

The **dragon head** warded off the evil spirits of the sea.

prow

oar holes

stern

rudder

The **keel**, fixed to the massive planks of the stem and stern, helped to stabilize the boat in rough waters.

The **mast** was made out of pine and rose to 18 to 20 m (60 to 66 ft) high on a 24-m-long (80-ft) longboat.

rising at the prow and stern. The Vikings believed that these figureheads protected the boats from the evil spirits that lurked out at sea. Longships could be anything between 13.5 and 24 m (45 and 80 ft) long. The vessels were sturdy and manoeuvrable for the rough conditions through which they sailed. Usually, they were powered by the single rectangular sail, but they could also be rowed by two rows of oarsmen, making them ideal both for sea travel and for exploring rivers.

that a chief was a leader among equals, rather than a ruler of inferiors, carried in it the germ of modern-day principles of democracy.

Pagans and Christians

In AD 829, the Christian **missionary** Saint Ansgar (801–65) arrived in Sweden. He founded a church and converted a few islanders. After two brief visits, he returned to Germany, where he became bishop of Hamburg. His arrival began two centuries of bitter struggle between Christianity and the Norse religion. The war-like beliefs of Viking society were very different from the meekness taught by the Christian missionaries.

Christian visitors to Scandinavia were particularly horrified by the Vikings' occasional practice of human sacrifice as part of their religion. Every nine years, celebrations were held at Uppsala in southern Sweden that centred on the sacrifice of nine victims. One visitor from Germany wrote that at the Sacred Grove at Uppsala, he saw the headless corpses of humans and dogs hanging from every tree.

Lund in Skåne was the seat of Sweden's – and Scandinavia's – first bishops. The cathedral's crypt holds the tomb of Sweden's patron saint, Saint Erik.

By the end of the 11th century, the temple at Uppsala had been destroyed and a church built on its site. In the early 12th century, Uppsala was made the centre of Swedish Christianity, and a British monk, Stephen, was appointed the first archbishop of Sweden. Christianity transformed Viking society. The Christian priests built churches and schools and set down Sweden's laws in writing.

For many centuries, however, the pagan beliefs and traditions lived on alongside the new Christian ones. **Rune** and picture stones (see pages 98–9) depicted Viking stories as well as Christian ones. And even after Sweden's rulers became Christians, they still liked to claim descent from the powerful fertility god, Freyr.

The spread of Christianity

During the 10th and 11th centuries, missionaries from Britain and Germany sought to convert the peoples of Scandinavia to Christianity. While the southern parts of Sweden and Norway became Christian towards the end of the 10th century, many northern areas remained pagan until well into the 14th century or longer.

The first Swedish kingdom

Until around AD 1000, what we now call Sweden was made up of separate, independent territories. During the 11th century, however, the territories began to unite. Sweden, Norway and Denmark emerged as separate kingdoms. Olof Skötonung (died 1022) became the first king of Sweden whose name is recorded. Olof was also the first Swedish king to be baptized.

Starting in the middle of the 12th century, Sweden was torn by endless power struggles between two families, the Sverkers and the Eriks. From 1160 to 1250, the crown passed back and forth between the two. King Erik Jedvarssen, a Sverker, was the most famous king of the period. In 1157, he led a crusade into Finland to convert the Finnish people, who had so far resisted the efforts of the Christian missionaries. In 1160, a Danish claimant to the Swedish throne killed Erik at Uppsala. A century later, Erik became the patron saint of Sweden.

Despite the upheavals surrounding the Swedish kingship, the country generally remained stable. The various counties of the kingdom remained powerful and continued to elect the king, who had his seat in Uppsala.

By the late 13th century, however, the Swedish kings began to impose their power more forcibly on the counties. They built royal castles throughout the kingdom to act as centres for royal administration. Over time, the **monarchy** established enough authority to create a central government, imposing and enforcing laws throughout the whole kingdom. In 1249, the Swedish kings completed the conquest of Finland.

At this time, Swedish society was organized along feudal lines. Feudalism was a system of organizing society that was common throughout medieval Europe. Under feudalism, society was divided into three broad classes – the clergy (priests), nobles and peasants. The nobles promised to serve the king, who in return gave them lands and control over peasants.

King Magnus
In 1280, King Magnus Ladulås (reigned 1275–90) was able to gain more power than any other previous Swedish king had enjoyed or would do so for another 300 years. Sweden's nobles pledged allegiance to him and promised to fight for him. Magnus also appointed a council of representatives from the clergy and the nobles. To further reinforce his power, the king ruled that the nobles and other leaders had to have

During the Middle Ages, Swedish stonemasons made numerous fonts for Sweden's new churches. Fonts were used for baptism, one of the most important Christian rites. This baptismal font is from Loderup in Skåne.

his permission even to meet together. This made it difficult for them to plan a conspiracy against him.

Magnus's surname Ladulås means 'barn lock'. This refers to the king's ban on the tradition that nobles could travel from castle to castle and be supported by the peasants who farmed the castle lands. After this change, the peasants were able to keep their food for themselves, locked away in their barns.

A united Scandinavia

After Magnus's death in 1290, the king's three sons and a group of powerful men, led by the king's former marshal (military leader), Torgil Knuttsen, fought among themselves for power. They divided Sweden into separate kingdoms again, until eventually the nobles seized power and restored a single, united monarchy. They made Magnus Eriksson (1316–74), the three-year-old son of a Swedish duke and a Norwegian princess, who was already king of Norway, king of Sweden, too.

Magnus ruled from 1319 to 1363. During his reign, he signed a treaty with the Russian principality of Novgorod establishing their shared borders in eastern and northern Finland. This left almost all of the Scandinavian **Peninsula** – with the exception of the Danish provinces of Blekinge and Skåne in present-day southern Sweden – in the hands of a single ruler.

Saint Bridget

Bridget was born in about 1303, the daughter of a governor of the province of Uppland. From a very early age, she experienced mystical visions. She later married the governor of another province and raised eight children. After the death of her husband in 1344, she went into the countryside near the shores of Lake Vättern to devote herself to prayer and reflection. She told her visions to the abbot of the nearby monastery of Alvastra, who wrote them down in Latin.

In 1350, Bridget travelled to Rome. There she remained for the rest of her life, leaving only to make a religious pilgrimage to the Holy Land (Palestine) in the company of one of her children, who later became Saint Catherine of Sweden (c.1331–81).

In 1370, fulfilling a command given to her in a vision, Bridget founded a strict order of nuns and monks – the Brigittine Order. After a life of sheltering the poor and homeless, Bridget died in 1372. In recognition of her holiness, the church made her a saint in 1391.

The Hanseatic League

During the 14th and 15th centuries, Sweden's prosperity was threatened by the powerful Hanseatic League (Hansa). The Hanseatic League was a loose association of trading cities in northern Germany, led by Lübeck and Cologne. The league was governed by a group made up of traders from the various member cities.

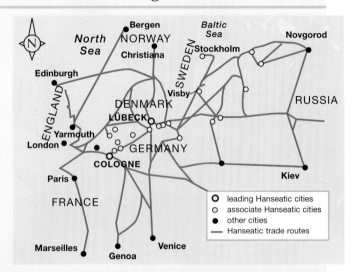

Through its valuable trade, the league came to dominate the whole of the Baltic region, gaining control of the Russian fur trade, the Flemish wool trade and the Swedish fish trade. The Hanseatic traders developed a distinctive type of ship, called a cog, that was designed to carry as much cargo as possible.

The Hanseatic traders established trading stations throughout the Baltic. Sometimes, they even founded settlements. In Sweden, the German newcomers settled alongside the Swedes around modern-day Stockholm and particularly on the island of Gotland. There, the town of Visby developed as an important trading centre for valuable commodities, including German beer, French wine, Indian and west African spices, English wool and Russian furs.

The German settlers tended to remain aloof from Swedish society. For example, when the Danish king attacked Visby in 1361, the Hanseatic settlers locked the Gotlanders out of the city gates and allowed them to be massacred. Nevertheless, the German settlers exerted a powerful influence on Swedish culture and society for some 200 years until the middle of the 16th century. German architecture and sculpture were fashionable, and the Swedish language absorbed many German words.

In general, Sweden and the Swedes did not prosper from the Hanseatic League. The country remained dependent on agriculture, and although advances such as crop rotation and improved tools helped farming to develop during this time, Sweden suffered a long period of economic decline.

Magnus's reign was troubled by plague and war. At this time, bubonic plague, popularly known as the Black Death, ravaged Europe, killing millions. In Sweden, the disease decreased the population dramatically, possibly by as much as one-third, and there were not enough people to work on the country's farms.

Magnus was also at war with Denmark over the provinces of Skåne and Blekinge. In 1361, the Danish king, Valdemar Atterdag (c.1320–75), landed in Gotland and slaughtered its inhabitants. Valdemar forced Magnus to marry his son Håkon, the king of Norway, to his daughter Margaret (1353–1412). Soon after, the Swedish royal council deposed Magnus.

The Union of Kalmar

In 1389, the royal council proclaimed Margaret the Queen of Sweden. By the deaths of both her father and husband, she had already become the ruler of both Denmark and Norway. In 1397, Margaret officially linked her three kingdoms under the Union of Kalmar, named after a mighty castle on Sweden's east coast. She appointed her grandnephew Erik of Pomerania (c.1381–1459) as king, although she held on to power until her death.

In 1397, the castle at Kalmar, on the coast of Småland, became the scene of one of the most momentous events in Sweden's history – the proclamation of the Kalmar Union.

The Kalmar Union lasted for more than a hundred years. Many Swedes – both nobles and peasants alike – disliked the union, especially since it seemed to serve the interests mainly of Denmark. When Erik

gained real power after Margaret's death, he waged long wars to gain back the former Danish territory of Schleswig and imposed high taxes on his subjects to pay for his campaigns. His actions also angered the Hanseatic League, which set up a blockade on the union's trade. Sweden's economy was badly affected, sparking a famous rebellion (see box). In 1439, the nobles removed Erik from the throne.

Sweden's nobles were divided between those who wished to see an independent Sweden and those who favoured the Kalmar Union and the ties with Denmark. The former were led by the powerful Sture family. In 1471, Sten Sture (*c.*1440–1503) defeated the Danish king and the pro-unionists in the famous Battle of Brunkeberg, which took place within the very walls of Stockholm.

The Swedish unionists, led by the archbishop Gustav Trolle (1488–1535), continued to plot against the Stures. In 1520, the Danish king of the union, Christian II, invaded Sweden and had himself crowned king. Soon after, he beheaded 82 Swedish nobles on trumped-up charges of heresy and burnt their bodies. This cruel action came to be known as the 'Swedish Bloodbath'.

Engelbrekt Engelbrektsson

Sweden's first great national hero was the 15th-century nobleman Engelbrekt Engelbrektsson (*c.*1390–1436). The Swedes think of him as their national saviour, in much the same way the French consider Joan of Arc theirs.

Engelbrekt was a mine owner in Bergslagen, an area in modern Dalarna county. As everywhere in Sweden, the peasants and miners of Bergslagen were heavily taxed. In the summer of 1434, they revolted against the king, Erik of Pomerania, burning down the local castles. Engelbrekt quickly emerged as the revolt's leader and led his army to Stockholm. By November, Engelbrekt had forced the king to sign a peace treaty in which he promised reforms.

In 1436, when it was clear that Erik would not carry out his promises, Engelbrekt led another revolt. Once again, the people of Stockholm welcomed him as a hero, and once again the king promised reforms. At this point, however, a quarrel broke out among the rebels. An old enemy of Engelbrekt, Magnus Bengtsson, murdered him as he camped on an island on Lake Mälaren.

THE VASAS

The Swedes had had enough. Revolts against Danish rule broke out everywhere. One young nobleman, Gustav Vasa (*c.*1496–1560), tried to rouse the peasants of Dalarna to rebel but was forced to flee to Norway on skis when they proved reluctant. According to legend, the peasants soon changed their minds. They, too, set off on skis and, catching up with him, promised him their help. The event is still celebrated today in the annual Vasaloppet, a ski race in which thousands of Swedes take part. In 1523, Vasa marched on Stockholm with his peasant army, forcing the Danes to flee. The nobles elected him king, bringing the disastrous Kalmar Union to an end.

Gustav I Vasa proved to be one of Sweden's most brilliant monarchs. During his reign (1523–60), he laid down the foundations of many Swedish institutions, including its church, army and navy.

The Swedish king Gustav I Vasa – the first of the great Vasa dynasty that ruled Sweden from 1523 to 1818 – laid down many of the foundations of the modern Swedish nation.

By the late 16th century, many parts of northern Europe were officially Protestant. The Hapsburg empire was divided between Protestant and Catholic princes.

The Reformation

In the early 16th century, the religious movement called the **Reformation** swept through northern Europe. The Reformation challenged the supremacy of the Roman Catholic Church in Rome and taught a version of Christianity that valued simple faith and the reading of the Bible. One of its principal leaders was the German monk Martin Luther (1483–1546).

The Reformation

Roman Catholic areas
Protestant areas
– – – boundary of Hapsburg empire

NORWAY
SWEDEN
DENMARK
ENGLAND
NETHERLANDS
GERMAN STATES
POLAND
FRANCE
HUNGARY
ROME
N

Lutheranism remained Sweden's official religion until January 2000.

Like England's King Henry VIII, Gustav realized that by supporting the Reformation he could stop church interference in Sweden's affairs and increase his own power. The establishment of an independent church in Sweden – called the **Lutheran Church** after Martin Luther – also gave Gustav the opportunity to raise much-needed money by seizing and selling lands held by the Roman Catholic Church.

Gustav's adviser Olaus Petri (1493–1552) is often regarded as the father of the Swedish Reformation. In the early years of Gustav's reign, Petri translated the New Testament into Swedish and later wrote many books explaining Luther's ideas. Later, he also wrote *A Swedish Chronicle*, a history of Sweden up to 1520.

Strengthening the monarchy

Gustav Vasa's reforms encompassed much more than the church. He also strengthened the Swedish monarchy. It had always been elective, meaning that each time a king died or was overthrown, the nobility effectively took power and elected the new ruler. In 1544, Gustav Vasa made the crown hereditary, guaranteeing that it would pass down through his male heirs, from father to eldest son. Daughters could not succeed to the throne unless there were no other sons.

King Gustavus Adolph was a brilliant soldier and courtier. He spoke five languages and invented a new, easily manoeuvrable cannon.

The nobles objected bitterly to Vasa's move, which limited their influence and greatly increased the king's. Over the next 40 years, the nobility attempted several times to re-establish their power. During the reigns of his successors, Charles IX (reigned 1599–1611) and Gustav II Adolf, known as Gustavus Adolph (reigned 1611–32), however, the monarchy became even stronger.

'The Lion of the North'

Gustavus Adolph (1594–1632) was an ambitious ruler who entangled his country in Europe's wars. He was a brilliant soldier, winning battles against Denmark, Russia and Poland. His victories earned him the nickname 'The Lion of the North'. The French emperor Napoleon thought him the equal of some of the greatest military leaders of history, including Alexander the Great and Julius Caesar.

Gustavus Adolph also accomplished much at home, reforming Sweden's administrative system. He also imported money, merchants and architects from the Netherlands, then Protestant Europe's leading commercial and cultural centre. The Dutch influence is especially evident in the architecture of Göteborg, which the king founded.

In 1618, Europe's Thirty Years' War spread to Germany, where the Protestant princes fought their Catholic overlord, the Holy Roman emperor, in Vienna. In 1630, Gustavus intervened on the side of the German Protestants, leading an army south into central Europe. After a string of brilliant victories, Gustavus Adolph was killed in 1632 at the Battle of Lützen.

The end of the Vasas

After Gustavus's death, his daughter Christina (1626–89; see page 66) became Queen of Sweden. She was only six years old and, until she came of age, the country was ruled by Axel Oxelstierna, her father's chancellor. In 1654, Christina shocked Sweden by giving up her throne and becoming a Roman Catholic. She was the last of Gustav Vasa's direct descendants to rule Sweden.

Swedish intervention

In 1630, King Gustavus Adolph led his army south into Europe.

Queen Christina

As a girl, Christina was educated exactly as a boy would have been at the time. She learned many languages, read philosophy and liked to go hunting (below). By the time she came of age in 1644, she was a clever and cultured woman. She corresponded with the brilliant French philosopher René Descartes (1596–1650), to whom she confessed her growing doubts about the Protestant religion. After her **abdication** in 1654, she lived much of her life in Rome – the centre of the Roman Catholic Church – and died there in 1689.

Christina had named her cousin Charles, the son of the Count Palatine, as her heir. He became Charles X Gustav (reigned 1654–60), the first of a new branch of the Vasa royal family called the Palatinate. His son and successor, Charles XI (reigned 1660–97), carried out far-reaching reforms. He took back all the Crown's lands that had been sold to the nobles, leaving them impoverished and powerless. He also reorganized the army and gave farms to the officers and cottages to the foot soldiers. In so doing, he created a loyal army that could serve Sweden's growing empire.

The great power time

By the mid-17th century, Sweden's kings had used warfare to build up a mighty **empire** that encompassed many of the lands that surrounded the Baltic Sea. From Denmark, the Swedes won back the prosperous counties of Skåne, Halland, Blekinge and Gotland that now form the southern part of Sweden's mainland. From the Norwegians, the Swedes took the provinces of Bohuslän, Jämtland, Trondheim and Härjedalen. Other territories held by Sweden included Finland, parts of the present-day Baltic republics of Estonia, Latvia and Lithuania, and a number of provinces in northern Germany.

Sweden was now a formidable force in northern Europe, a rival to England, France and the Hapsburg empire. Its empire even reached North America, where Swedes founded a short-lived colony along the Delaware River in present-day Pennsylvania, New Jersey and Delaware.

Sweden did not have the natural resources to support its empire for long. With the exception of a few small ironworks and a copper mine, the country still depended on agriculture. In 1697, when the fifteen-year-old Charles XII (1682–1718) came to the throne, the empire began to collapse despite the king's determined efforts to keep it together. Charles fought against every other power in the Baltic, including Denmark and Russia, until his aggression prompted even the English to declare war on Sweden.

Charles XII died from a sniper's bullet while leading an attack against the Danes in Norway in 1718. In the Great Northern War (1700–21), the combined forces of Denmark, Russia and Poland defeated Sweden and stripped it of most of its counties across the Baltic Sea. Sweden's borders shrank to encompass little more than present-day Finland and Sweden.

The Swedish empire in 1658

Between 1560 and 1658, Sweden fought a series of wars against its neighbours. By 1658, Stockholm stood at the centre of a vast Baltic empire. Soon after, however, the empire began to crumble. Already in 1660, Sweden lost the recently won Norwegian province of Trondheim.

Swedish historians often call the early 18th century 'the Time of Freedom'.

LIBERTY AND ABSOLUTISM

After the death of Charles XII in 1718, the Swedish *Riksdag* (parliament) introduced a new **constitution** that reduced the king's power and placed more power in its own hands. The new king, Frederick I (reigned 1720–51), remained the head of state, but real power lay in the hands of the head of government – the chancellor.

For a few decades, the Swedish people enjoyed a period of relative peace and freedom. Only a privileged few, though, had the right to vote in the *Riksdag* elections. Government was in the hands of two main parties – the 'Caps' and the 'Hats' – who spent most of their time squabbling over power and did very little to carry out any real reforms or to improve the lot of the ordinary people.

The Gustavian period

In 1772, King Gustav III (reigned 1771–92) seized power back from the unpopular *Riksdag*. Seventeen years later, he took total (absolute) power. Despite this, Gustav proved a very popular monarch among the people. He founded hospitals and schools and granted freedom of worship.

Literature and painting flourished during Gustav III's reign. The king invited French scholars to live and work at his court and established the Swedish Academy to oversee the arts. The king 'improved' the Swedish language by removing many foreign words, and the first Swedish dictionary was published during his reign. It was during this time that Linnaeus (see page 36) wrote his ground-breaking works

Anders Celsius

Part of a large family of scientists, Anders Celsius (1701–44) was born in Uppsala. Like his father, he became a professor at the university. Celsius was probably the first to propose the theory – later proved to be true – that the Scandinavian landmass is rising from the ocean. His most celebrated invention was the Celsius thermometer, which measures temperature from 0° (the temperature at which water freezes) to 100° (the temperature at which water boils). Celsius's original thermometer, however, reversed these values.

on the classification of plants, and Anders Celsius (see box opposite) introduced the centigrade temperature scale.

For all his achievements, Gustav was unpopular with Sweden's nobility. In 1792, a former army officer named Johan Jakob Anckarström assassinated Gustav at the opera house in Stockholm where the king was attending a masked ball. The Italian composer Giuseppe Verdi later composed a famous opera (1859) about this event.

A foreign king

At the beginning of the 19th century, Europe was plunged into war as the French emperor, Napoleon, sought to extend his empire across the continent. During the wars, Sweden lost Finland to Russia. The Swedes were desperate for peace, and eventually a group of rebels overthrew the king in 1809, introducing a new constitution (see box). Many of the rebels admired the ideas of the French Revolution, summed up in the slogan 'Liberty, Equality and Brotherhood', and by the adventurous spirit of Napoleon's empire. In 1810, they invited one of Napoleon's marshals, Jean-Baptiste Bernadotte (1763–1844), to become heir to the Swedish throne.

Bernadotte, or Charles John, as he was now known, was a clever ruler. By careful diplomacy, he managed to obtain Norway as compensation for the loss of Finland. In 1814, Norway fought against Sweden to try to preserve its independence. Victorious, Sweden forced Norway into a union that lasted until 1905.

The ombudsman

One of Sweden's many gifts to the world is the role of ombudsman, which was created by the constitutional changes of 1809. The ombudsman is an official appointed by the government to investigate complaints against public authorities and officials. Any citizen can make a complaint to an ombudsman against any public body or government body or any official or civil servant. There are ombudsmen at all levels of Swedish government. The main ones, however, are the parliamentary ombudsmen elected by the *Riksdag*. Others deal with complaints against the justice system, ethnic or gender discrimination, children's rights, the rights of disabled people and press ethics.

Between 1810 and 1880, Sweden's population almost doubled. Swedes attribute this increase to 'peace, potatoes and vaccine'.

Jean-Baptiste Bernadotte ascended the throne in 1818 as Charles XIV and ruled until 1844. He was the first of the Bernadotte dynasty, and his descendants have kept the Swedish Crown in an unbroken line to the present day. Charles was a popular ruler who helped to restore stability and respect for Sweden by establishing its policy of **neutrality** and by encouraging co-operation between the Scandinavian countries.

Reform and emigration

Charles XIV's son and grandson, Oscar I (reigned 1844–59) and Charles XV (reigned 1859–72), were both zealous reformers. During their reigns, trade guilds were abolished, many taxes on **imports** and **exports** were lifted and a system of local government was set up. The most important reform took place in 1866, when Charles XV created a new parliament of two houses, rather like the House of Commons and the House of Lords in the United Kingdom. The 1866 reform effectively brought an end to the personal power of the Swedish monarch.

Despite these changes, Sweden remained a poor and backward country. About 90 per cent of the population still depended on agriculture for a living. When famine hit rural areas in 1867 and 1868, many Swedes decided to emigrate, mainly to North America, where they settled particularly in the Midwest in the USA. From the middle of the 19th century until 1930, some 1.5 million Swedes emigrated.

At home, many people began to demand more far-reaching changes. Swedish workers campaigned for better working conditions and pay, while Swedish women struggled to gain equality with men.

Relatives and friends in Göteborg wave farewell to emigrants leaving for England and America. This photograph was taken at the beginning of the 20th century.

SWEDEN IN THE 20TH CENTURY

During the first half of the 20th century, two world wars tore Europe apart. Sweden, however, held firm to a policy of neutrality, meaning that it avoided taking part in military conflicts. During World War One (1914–18), Sweden, along with Norway and Denmark, was neutral. Some Swedes, though, volunteered as Red Cross workers.

Democracy and neutrality

Meanwhile, the country was undergoing more reforms. During the first years of the 20th century, the labour movement argued for increased political power for ordinary people. Their ideas were known as social **democracy** and had an increasing effect on government policy. The right to vote was granted for men in 1909 and for women in 1921 – seven years before all women in the United Kingdom were entitled to vote. The Social Democrats became increasingly influential until, in 1932, they became the governing party.

When World War Two broke out in 1939, Sweden again declared itself neutral. To protect its neutrality, the Social Democrats formed a **coalition** with other parties. During the early war years, Sweden continued to trade with both sides fighting the war. In order to prevent a German invasion of Sweden, the prime minister Per Albin Hansson (1885–1946) signed an agreement with the German leader Adolf Hitler, allowing German troops to travel through Sweden to occupied Norway. The agreement was very unpopular with Swedes and was ended in 1943.

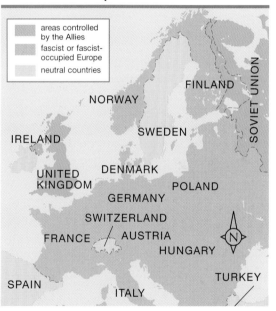

Europe in 1942

areas controlled by the Allies
fascist or fascist-occupied Europe
neutral countries

During World War Two, Sweden was one of the few European countries and the only Scandinavian country to remain neutral or unoccupied.

Blessed are the peacemakers

Sweden has repeatedly used its neutral status to act as a highly effective peace-broker in various conflicts. One of the best-known non-military heroes of World War Two was Raoul Wallenberg (1912–47), a Swedish diplomat in Budapest, capital of Hungary. Wallenberg issued official Swedish passports, and thus protection, to Jews and other people in danger of Nazi persecution. It was to Count Bernadotte of Wisborg (1895–1948), the nephew of Sweden's King Gustav V, that the Nazi leader Heinrich Himmler handed the official Nazi surrender in 1945, and it was the count who, as part of the negotiations to end the war, obtained the release of prisoners from concentration camps. The buses that carried the released prisoners out of Germany came to be known as 'Bernadotte's white buses'.

Today, Sweden is still respected as a peacemaker. The Swedish **Nobel Peace Prize** (left), first given in 1901, remains the world's greatest award for a contribution to peace and reconciliation.

After the war, the Social Democrats resumed office, with Per Albin Hansson as prime minister. During the 1940s and 1950s, the Social Democrats introduced the social reforms they had planned before the war. The **welfare state** they put in place provided education, health care, pensions, insurance and welfare payments designed to provide essential services for all citizens, regardless of their wealth, age or background. In Sweden the system was known as the *Folkhem* (People Home). The vast majority of Swedes were prepared to pay high taxes for the new reforms.

The oil crisis

In 1973, dramatic increases in the price of oil brought a worldwide economic crisis. As in virtually all other industrialized countries, unemployment in Sweden rose rapidly. The crisis brought a change of government in the 1976 elections, when the Social Democrats briefly lost power to a coalition of conservative parties, led by the chairman of the Centre Party, Thorbjörn Fälldin. The coalition's rule, however, was dogged by the issue of Sweden's nuclear-power plants (see page 88).

In the 1982 parliamentary elections, the Social Democrats were returned to power, with Olof Palme as prime minister. The new government took measures to improve Sweden's economy. International trade increased sharply in 1983 and in subsequent years, enabling Sweden to balance its national budget. The return to economic stability prompted the government to begin another massive expansion of public services.

Assassination

Sweden enjoyed a reputation as a peaceful, civilized and fair country. The atmosphere was so calm that even important people such as the prime minister could walk the streets in safety without a bodyguard. On 28 February 1986, the people were deeply shocked when Prime Minister Olof Palme was assassinated on the street in Stockholm as he and his wife returned from an evening at the cinema. No one is sure who carried out the assasination.

Another Social Democrat, Ingvar Carlsson, succeeded Palme as Sweden's prime minister and continued to carry out traditional Social Democratic policies. In the late 1980s, economic decline meant that it was increasingly difficult for the government to afford to pay for the reforms. As the economic crisis deepened, Swedes

Swedes remember Prime Minister Olof Palme with great affection. In a largely peaceful country, his murder in 1986 sent shock waves through Swedish society.

grew dissatisfied, and in 1991 they voted for a non-Social Democratic coalition government led by Carl Bildt, the leader of the Moderate Party.

Bildt, however, made little headway against rising unemployment, the growing budget deficit and the increasing **national debt** – the very problems he had been elected to combat. The interruption in the rarely broken chain of Social Democratic governments lasted only one term. In 1994, the Social Democrats took power again, though without an overall majority.

European Union

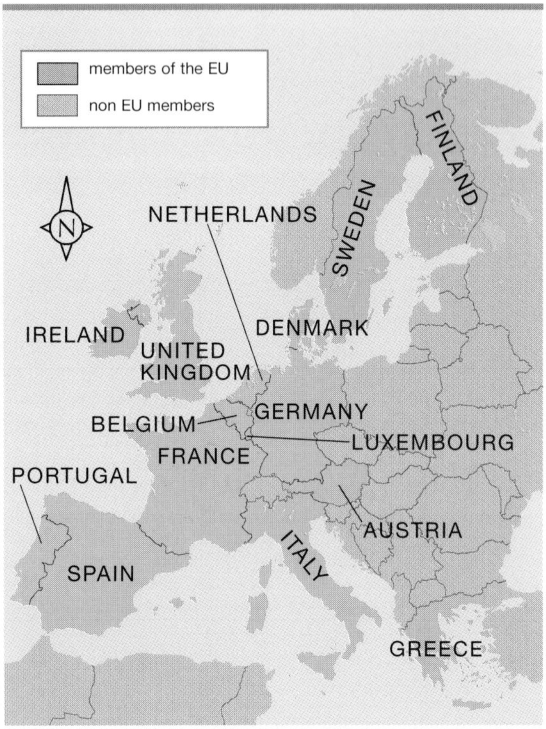

Legend:
- members of the EU
- non EU members

Map labels: FINLAND, SWEDEN, NETHERLANDS, IRELAND, DENMARK, UNITED KINGDOM, BELGIUM, GERMANY, FRANCE, LUXEMBOURG, PORTUGAL, AUSTRIA, ITALY, SPAIN, GREECE

Sweden joined the European Union (EU) in 1995, along with Austria and Finland. There are currently fifteen members of the EU, and other countries are due to join.

Sweden and the European Union

On 1 January 1995, Sweden joined the European Union (EU) – a group of European countries that work together on many economic, social and political issues. Many Swedes were unsure about how closely they wished to become integrated with their fellow Europeans. In the initial referendum (national vote) held on the issue, only 52.3 per cent of Swedes voted in favour of joining the union.

In 1998, elections at home underlined Sweden's uncertainty about Europe. The Social Democrats won power again but with even fewer votes than they had won in the 1994 elections. On the other hand, parties like the Moderate Party that questioned the value of further integration into Europe made strong gains. In 1999, Sweden decided not to join the European single currency, the euro, when it was introduced. In 2002, the Social Democrats were again re-elected to power, this time with a slightly increased majority.

The current king of Sweden, Charles XVI Gustav (reign 1973–), rides out of the Royal Palace with his wife, Queen Silvia. The royal family is very popular in Sweden.

SWEDEN'S SYSTEM OF GOVERNMENT

Like the United Kingdom, Sweden is a **constitutional monarchy**. The monarch (king or queen) is head of state but the country is governed under the principles of a constitution. Sweden's 1974 constitution (see box) removed all political power from the monarch, and today the king or queen remains head of state but has only ceremonial duties.

Until 1971, the Swedish *Riksdag* (parliament) comprised two houses. Now it is a one-house legislature. Every four years, the Swedish electorate – those entitled to vote, which in Sweden is everyone eighteen years and over – takes part in national elections. They vote for the party of their choice, and the parties allot the 349 seats of the *Riksdag* in proportion to the number of votes they have won. This electoral system is called proportional representation. In Sweden, a party has to gain at least 4 per cent of the vote to get any seats at all.

The constitution

Today's Swedish constitution was introduced in 1974. Its basic idea is that all public power comes from the people, who select their members of parliament in free elections. Some of its principles are listed below:

• Only the *Riksdag* can pass laws.

• The government – that is, the prime minister and the Cabinet – is appointed by and is answerable to the *Riksdag*.

• The monarch remains head of state but his or her functions are purely ceremonial.

• An amendment to the constitution changed the order of succession, introducing equal rights of inheritance for men and women. This means that Princess Victoria is now heir to the throne, rather than her younger brother Carl Philip.

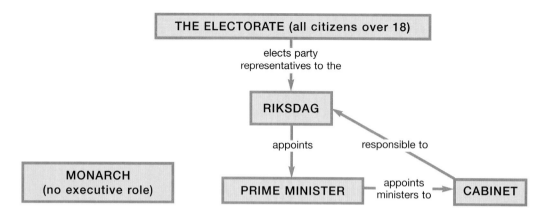

The administration

An important position in the *Riksdag* is that of the
Speaker. After an election, the Speaker confers with
party leaders and then proposes a new prime minister
(*statsminister*). The members of parliament (MPs) then
vote for or against the proposed prime minister. If an
absolute majority votes against the proposal, it fails.
Otherwise, it is approved. If it is approved, the Speaker
formally appoints the prime minister, who then
appoints all his or her Cabinet (*regering*) – the group of
ministers that lead the country's administration.

The Swedish Cabinet has 22 ministers in all. Besides
the prime minister and deputy prime minister, there are
thirteen heads of ministry (*departementeschef*). There
are ministers, for example, of justice, foreign affairs,
defence, and health and social affairs. Since the 1998

THE SWEDISH PARLIAMENT IN 2002

Riksdag
349 members • last election 2002 • elections held every 4 years

Party	%
Social Democratic Party	40%
Moderate Party	15%
People's Party	13%
Christian Democrat Party	9%
others	23%

election, half the members of the Cabinet have been women – something that is still unusual among governments throughout the world. The ministries devote most of their time to preparing new government bills.

Law enforcement is handled by about 100 central administrative agencies and the 21 county administrations. Each county also has an elected council that levies an income tax and takes responsibility for health care. In addition, there are 288 local **municipalities** covering the country. Each has an elected council that collects an income tax and administers local public services, including schools, housing and care for children and the elderly.

A distinctive feature of Swedish political life is the commitment to the principle of open government. While the government can keep certain documents secret if they involve national security, other documents must be made available to the general public.

Sweden has a strong national defence system. All Swedish males must do military service. Every year, about 50,000 young men report for duty, of whom 35,000 are chosen for basic training. Usually completed by the age of eighteen, the training lasts between seven and fifteen months.

The Swedish parliament building (Riksdagshuset) stands on the small island of Helgeandsholmen in Stockholm's Gamla Stan (Old Town).

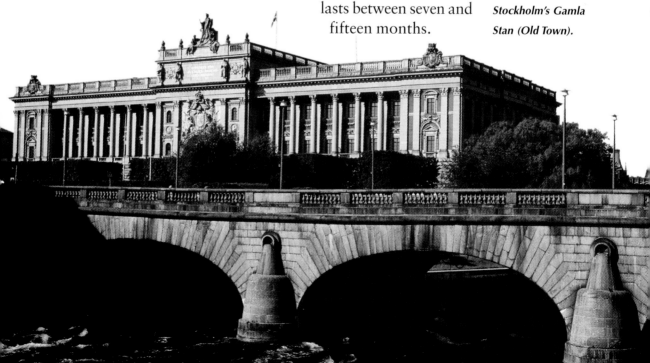

The economy

'Competitiveness abroad and a high living standard at home make the Swedish experience well worth studying.'

US Senate report

Sweden's present-day prosperity is one of the success stories of the 20th century. Until the end of the 19th century, most of the population made its living from the land, even though the country was rich in **natural resources**, such as timber and minerals.

In the 20th century, Sweden **industrialized** rapidly. Swedish scientists and engineers emerged as some of the most brilliant in the world. Designers, too, worked to produce goods that were not only good to look at but were also practical to use. Above all, Sweden's industrialists drew on the country's heritage as a great trading nation in order to **export** their products.

Today, the government works closely with employers and employees to improve not only economic performance but also the welfare of everyone. As a result, the Swedes have some of the best welfare rights in the world. However, they also pay some of the highest rates of taxes.

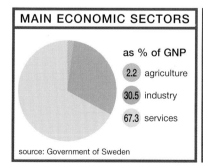

MAIN ECONOMIC SECTORS

as % of GNP

2.2 agriculture
30.5 industry
67.3 services

source: Government of Sweden

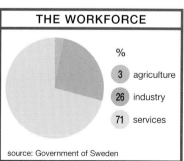

THE WORKFORCE

%

3 agriculture
26 industry
71 services

source: Government of Sweden

Logs on a tree plantation await transportation to a sawmill. Timber, pulp and paper products account for just under 15 per cent of Sweden's exports.

Over half of Sweden is covered by forest, while one-third is mountainous or covered by lakes and marshes.

MAIN ECONOMIC SECTORS

Traditionally, Sweden's abundance of natural resources has underpinned the country's economy and provided its industries with valuable raw materials. Today, however, the country's prosperity is dependent on its service and manufacturing industries. Because Sweden's population and therefore its home market are small, it is important for Swedish businesses to sell their products overseas.

HOW SWEDEN USES ITS LAND

high mountains
crop land
forest
pasture

Forests and minerals

Sweden has a wealth of natural resources. The country's forests provide timber for building homes and furniture and for export, while fast-flowing rivers produce **hydroelectricity**.

Although Sweden has no oil or coal resources, it does have many other mineral deposits, found mostly in the north. Mines extract iron, copper and silver, and Sweden is one of the world's leading producers of lead and zinc. Sweden also possesses 80 per cent of Europe's uranium deposits.

Cows and reindeer

Despite Sweden's large size, only about 7 per cent of the land is suitable for agriculture. There are important differences, too, between farming in the north and in the south of the country. The growing period in southern Sweden is almost 100 days longer than in the north. The farms in the northern parts of the country and in densely forested areas are generally smaller than those located in the flat country in the south.

Animal farming is more important than cereal farming in Sweden. Dairy cows are found throughout the country (see page 6). The pasture lands of the south are dotted with a distinctive breed of red-and-white cows that are famous for their high milk yield. In the mountainous north, there are hardier breeds; the cows here are often horned and are white with black spots. Numbers of dairy cows have decreased in recent years. In 1960, there were some 1.6 million dairy cows in Sweden; in 1995, there were only 490,000. Milk yields, however, have improved.

Herds of reindeer graze in the northern half of the country. Under Swedish law, only the **Sami** people have the right to herd reindeer. Reindeer herding is organized in Sami villages, where the reindeer owners work together. There are two forms of reindeer herding: forest reindeer herding and mountain reindeer herding. The forest Sami villagers carry on reindeer herding in the forest area all year round, while the mountain Sami villagers migrate with the herds from lowland winter grazing areas to summer grazing areas in the mountains.

Crops are grown mostly in the south and include barley, sugar beet, rape and vegetables. In the north, potatoes and hay are the main crops. Sweden's agriculture has changed greatly in the last 50 years. Meadows and open pastures have been ploughed up or planted with forest. Hedges have been torn down to make bigger

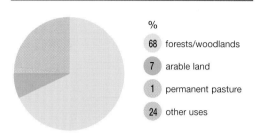

LAND USE

%
68 forests/woodlands
7 arable land
1 permanent pasture
24 other uses

source: Government of Sweden

This chart shows the percentages of Sweden's available land given over to various uses.

Sami herders often use a white reindeer to attract other reindeer in order to herd them.

fields, and the use of fertilizers and pesticides has increased enormously. Such changes have resulted in reduced **biodiversity** – that is, the variety of animal and plant species – in the agricultural landscape. Experts think that about one-fifth of species that lived in Sweden's fields, meadows and pastures has been lost or is threatened.

Forest products

Wood has been one of humankind's most important raw materials since prehistoric times. Nowadays, wood is processed and used for a variety of products.

Wood products are goods that are generally recognizable as wood, such as furniture or posts. Fibre products, such as paper, are made from the fibre of wood. Wood can be broken into its chemical parts and moulded to make items such as piano keys or table-tennis balls. Alternatively, it can simply be used as fuel.

Using the forests wisely

Sweden's forests cover some 68 per cent of the land and are one of the country's most valuable resources. Traditionally, wood was used for building houses and ships and as fuel for blast furnaces in the mining industry. Farmers cut down trees in the lean winter months and used their farm horses to transport the felled trees.

Since the 15th century, when the country's first sawmill was opened, the forest industry has expanded a great deal. During the 19th century, timber became a major export. Much of it, for example, went to Britain, where it provided fuel for the country's growing industry. Today, forestry is a high-tech industry with a small and highly skilled workforce. **Investments** in new pulp and paper mills are the largest industrial investments in Sweden.

Many other industries are dependent at least in part on forestry. For example, mechanical engineering companies develop and produce new machinery for mechanical and chemical pulping and paper production. The forest industry also helps support Sweden's transportation network, which carries the timber and wood products around the country and overseas. This gives jobs to a large number of transportation companies, from the national railway company to numerous haulage contractors. It also gives a boost to the lorry manufacturers Volvo and Scania.

The Swedish government tries to make sure that Sweden's forests are exploited wisely. The National Board of Forestry oversees the forestry industry, ensuring that productivity goes hand in hand with biodiversity.

Sweden is the third-largest producer of forest products in the world after Canada and the USA.

Fishing in salt water and fresh water

Unlike other Scandinavian countries, such as Norway and Denmark, Sweden has only a small fishing industry. In 1996, the total catch was about a quarter of that of its mighty fishing neighbour, Norway. About three-quarters of the catch is exported.

Göteborg is the main fishing port. Fishing boats land their North Sea catches of cod, mackerel and shark, and traders sell these saltwater fish from gleaming, ice-packed stalls in the city's indoor markets. The Baltic Sea is less salty than the North Sea and is home to different varieties of fish. The catch here includes pike, perch, sea trout and salmon. Freshwater salmon is also farmed in inland rivers and lakes.

Sami fishermen bring in their nets at Lake Jukkasjärvi in Norrbotten. Although traditionally reindeer herders, Sami people today also make their living by fishing, farming and many other kinds of work.

MAJOR INDUSTRIES

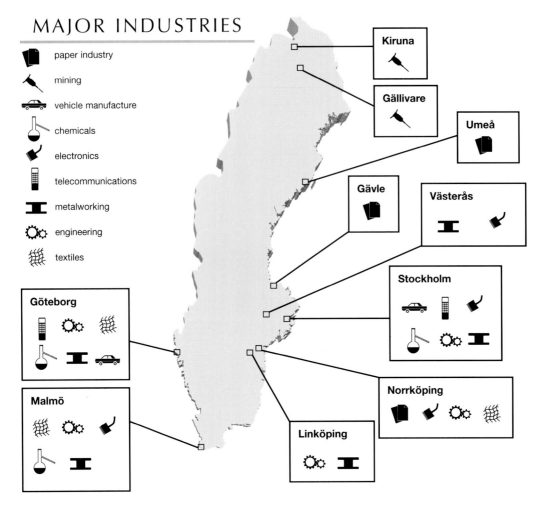

paper industry

mining

vehicle manufacture

chemicals

electronics

telecommunications

metalworking

engineering

textiles

Kiruna

Gällivare

Umeå

Gävle

Västerås

Stockholm

Göteborg

Malmö

Norrköping

Linköping

Sweden's industry is centred on its three major cities – Stockholm, Malmö and Göteborg. Other, smaller cities are usually home to specialized industries, such as paper production.

Industrial giants

Despite its small population of about 9 million, Sweden is one of the world's great industrial nations. In 1999, its industrial output was worth some £42,500 million – the 20th biggest in the world. Sweden's neighbours Norway and Finland ranked 27th and 32nd in the world, respectively.

Most of Sweden's companies are privately owned. The powerful Wallenberg family, for example, owns or part-owns many important industries as well the country's largest bank. The government tries to encourage industry by having a low business tax rate.

Since Viking times, Sweden's strength has always been its ability to trade, and today's industrial companies are geared towards exports. The first true multinational company was Swedish. The 19th-century Swedish manufacturer Alfred Nobel (1833–96) owned some 90 explosives factories in twenty countries all over the world.

Today, many Swedish companies are international household names, including the construction giant Skanska; Ikea, the world's largest furniture retailer; Tetra Pak, the world leader in packaging for liquids; the telecommunications company Ericsson and the vehicle manufacturers Volvo and Saab-Scania (see box).

Swedish factories are friendly, comfortable places in which to work. Company bosses and trade unions work

Vehicle manufacture

Sweden's biggest industrial and export success has been in motor vehicles. There are two world-famous vehicle companies – Volvo and Saab-Scania.

Volvo, which is based in Göteborg, makes cars that are famous for their performance and safety as much as for their sleek design. The company was founded in the 1920s when six engineers determined that they would build a Swedish car that would rival the cars made by

Ford. In the 1950s, Volvo began to compete directly with Ford, exporting vehicles to the USA. By the 1990s, Volvos were among the biggest-selling cars in North America.

Saab-Scania, based in Stockholm county, produces not only luxury cars, such as the 1999 convertible model below, but also lorries and coaches. In the 1960s, the company began exporting lorries to Australia and became the largest lorry company there.

together to achieve high productivity and good working conditions. The difference in pay between junior and senior members of a company is much less than in many other Western countries.

The picture is not all rosy, however. At the end of the 1990s, Swedish companies faced a crisis. Fierce international competition led to a wave of mergers and take-overs. A merger occurs when two equally powerful companies decide to join; a take-over happens when a stronger company buys a weaker one. No part of industry seemed safe. The vehicle division of Volvo was sold to the US company Ford for £4000 million. Other Swedish companies have moved out of their home country. Ericsson, for example, moved to London.

Glassware

Sweden is famous not only for its hi-tech industries but also for small-scale, craft-based products, such as furniture and glass. Sweden's first glassworks – called Kosta Buda – was opened in the 18th century in Småland, where the dense forests provided ample timber for the glass furnaces. Because there was no native tradition of glass-blowing, the first craftspeople had to be brought from Bohemia in central Europe. The Kosta Buda glassworks pioneered the manufacture of crystal, which is glass with a very high lead content. Småland is still the heart of the glass industry.

One of the most famous of Sweden's glass manufacturers is Orrefors. The company began by making ordinary things such as windowpanes and bottles. In 1913, however, the company began to specialize in fine tableware and decorative pieces. In today's glass industry, large manufacturers of mass-produced glassware exist side by side with small workshops that specialize in unique, handmade pieces, such the ones shown below.

THE SWEDES AT WORK

Most Swedish people work hard and are proud of their jobs. Telephone directories list a person's profession next to his or her name. Nevertheless, quality of life is very important. Swedes rarely work overtime and enjoy at least five weeks' holiday. They are entitled to sick and unemployment pay and paternity and maternity leave.

Working life is seen as a creative experience. Companies encourage their employees to train and to contribute their own ideas. Unions are very powerful in Sweden, but they are willing to work with management to solve problems and make improvements. In many other countries, unions and bosses are often at loggerheads.

There are problems, however. The high taxes paid by Swedish people often result in unwillingness to do extra paid work or take on higher-paid work with more responsibility. Many talented professionals go overseas in pursuit of higher salaries. Some people, too, take unfair advantage of the generous sick pay by taking time off work without good reason. In recent years, too, Sweden's high labour costs have been in danger of making Swedish goods uncompetitive. Some companies have had to lay off workers.

Sweden's excellent childcare system enables many people who would otherwise have to stay at home to look after their children to go out to work. This man is looking after children in a government-run day-care centre in central Stockholm.

In the car-making company Volvo, workers take an average of 27 sick days every year.

ENERGY: THE NUCLEAR DILEMMA

Sweden has no coal or oil. Until the 1970s, the country relied on hydroelectric power and **imported** oil to meet its electricity needs. In the 1970s, however, oil shortages and environmental concerns about the building of dams on Sweden's rivers pushed the government into using nuclear energy. Politicians hoped that in this way the country would be able to become self-sufficient in generating electrical power.

The first working nuclear reactor was built at Oskarshamn on Sweden's south-east coast, followed by others on the west and south coasts. Not everybody was happy about this development, especially since one of the reactors was built only about 20 kilometres (12 miles) from Malmö. In 1980, strict restrictions were placed on the nuclear industry. In 1986, fallout from the Chernobyl nuclear accident in Ukraine affected Sweden badly (see page 31) and turned more people against nuclear energy.

At present, however, Sweden remains a leading producer of nuclear power. Today, very little oil is imported into the country, and nuclear energy meets 43 per cent of Sweden's energy needs. Sweden tries to make its power plants as safe as possible. A special ship collects the radioactive spent fuel rods from each reactor and takes them to an underground storage facility. Eventually, the cooled rods will be sealed into copper blocks and buried deep under rock within the Earth.

Nevertheless, the nuclear programme is restricted to a maximum of twelve reactors and is due to end in 2010. Closures of plants have already begun. The government wants to develop other ways to generate electrical power, such as solar power, and to expand the hydroelectric programme. It is also trying to cut back Sweden's demand for energy. For example, new homes have to be built with energy conservation in mind. In the meantime, Sweden will have to import more electrical power from its neighbours, such as Germany and Denmark, and this will certainly include electricity generated by nuclear power.

Despite public concern, nuclear-generated electricity is used to meet 43 per cent of Sweden's energy needs. Hydroelectric power provides most of the rest of the country's energy needs.

ENERGY SOURCES

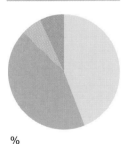

%

44 hydroelectricity

43 nuclear power

6 oil, gas, coal and diesel

7 other

source: Government of Sweden

MAIN TRADING PARTNERS

EXPORTS

%

10.8	Germany
9.2	UK
8.9	USA
7.9	Norway
5.9	Netherlands
57.3	others

source: Government of Sweden

IMPORTS

%

16.7	Germany
9.5	UK
7.7	Netherlands
6	Norway
5	Denmark
55.1	others

TRADE AND TRADING PARTNERS

Historically, Sweden has always been a great trading nation. The Vikings were industrious traders as well as fierce warriors, and since medieval times, Sweden's ports, such as Visby and Stockholm, were important merchant cities on the Baltic trading routes (see page 60). Today, the Swedish economy is heavily dependent on exports, which account for about one-third of the country's gross national product (GNP). Sweden has a current account surplus – that is, it exports more than it imports.

Traditionally, Sweden's chief exports were its raw materials, including timber and iron ore, and semi-manufactured products, such as pulp and steel. In the 20th century, however, there was a shift towards industrial products, such as vehicles and electronic goods. Nevertheless, wood and paper products still remain the country's second-largest export.

Sweden's chief trading partners are Germany, the United Kingdom, the USA, Norway and Denmark. Sweden is a member of the **European Union** (EU) and about 60 per cent of its trade is within the EU.

Sweden's membership in the European Union (EU) means that most of its trade is with other EU nations.

Sweden exports more than it imports. This gives the country what is known as a current account surplus.

EXPORTS (£000 m)		IMPORTS (£000 m)	
machinery and electricals	17.5	machinery and electricals	12.6
wood and paper	7.9	chemicals	4.9
transport equipment	7.4	transport equipment	4.1
chemicals	4.9	food, drink and tobacco	2.9
iron and steel products	2.9	mineral fuels	2.8
total (including others)	52.8	total (including others)	41.7

source: Government of Sweden

TRANSPORTATION

Sweden's extensive road and rail network means that most parts of the country are easily accessible. The building of the Öresund Link between Malmö and Copenhagen means that transportation between Sweden and Denmark is easier than ever.

Björkliden
Kiruna
Gällivare
Östersund
Umeå
Örnsköldsvik
Änge
Sundsvall
Borlänge
Karlstad
Örebro   STOCKHOLM
Göta
Canal
Norrköping
Göta
Canal
Linköping
Göteborg
Visby
Borås
Gotland
Jönköping
Öland
Kalmar
Helsingborg
Malmö   Kristianstad
COPENHAGEN
Öresund Link   Trelleborg

——— major roads
+++++ railways
✈ international airport
⛴ --- ferry route
---- waterway

TRANSPORTATION

Sweden has one of the most advanced transportation networks in the world. There are fast, uncrowded roads and a cheap, efficient railway network. Ferries shuttle between the islands and across the Baltic to Finland and Denmark. Much of the transportation system, including the national airline, is owned by the government.

By water

Sweden began as a great seafaring nation. The Viking longships of the peoples of **Scandinavia** carried them all over Europe and even reached the Americas. Sweden's three biggest cities – Stockholm, Göteborg and Malmö – are also three of Scandinavia's greatest ports. Until the 19th century, travelling by water remained the prime means of transportation, particularly in summer when the Baltic was free of ice. Engineers built numerous waterways, among them the famous Göta Canal (see box opposite).

By the 20th century, the canals of inland Sweden fell into disuse as more and better roads and railways were built. Göteborg and Stockholm are still busy ports, however. Along the Norrland coast, the forestry industry has its own harbours where timber is loaded onto cargo ships and shipped to sawmills. In winter, though, many harbours, including Stockholm's, freeze over, and icebreakers have to work hard to keep shipping routes clear. Ferries carry passengers and cars to Gotland and

The Göta Canal

Swedish kings, engineers and business people long dreamed of building a canal that would connect Sweden's west coast with the Baltic Sea. Finally, in 1810, engineer Baltzar von Platen started work on the project. For 22 years, some 58,000 men laboured to complete the 579-km (360-mile) canal. By 1832, the waterway from Göteborg to Stockholm was navigable and became a vital transportation route for Sweden's iron and timber.

With the building of the first railway across Sweden in the early 1860s, the canal seemed to have become obsolete. Some boat owners, however, believed that the canal could still flourish. The captain of one steamer, Erik Thorsell, decided to carry passengers on the canal and marketed the voyages as a tourist attraction. By the 1880s, Thorsell's company operated eleven tourist vessels. During World War One (1914–18), when the Baltic shipping routes became dangerous, the canal steamers provided a safe means of cargo transportation between Göteborg and Stockholm. Today, thousands of tourists enjoy summer cruises on the peaceful canal.

Many famous people have travelled on the canal, including the Danish writer Hans Christian Andersen and the Norwegian playwright Henrik Ibsen. Sweden's kings have been frequent users of the canal. In 1922, King Gustav V celebrated the centenary of the western section of the canal. Three newly painted canal steamers flying the Swedish flag carried the royal party along the canal. The local people waved and applauded from the canal banks.

MAIN TOURIST
ARRIVALS

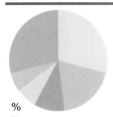

%

29	Germany
19	Norway
10	Denmark
7	eastern Europe
6	Finland
29	others

source: Government
of Sweden

Most overseas visitors
to Sweden come
from Germany and
neighbouring countries
in Scandinavia.

other islands, while in summer in the Stockholm **Archipelago,** a fleet of distinctive white boats criss-crosses the blue water.

Taking the train

The government began building railways in the 1850s, and today they are still mostly publicly owned. Swedish State Railways (Statens Järnväger, or SJ) runs 9821 kilometres (6102 miles) of track. The network reaches as far north as Björkliden on the Norwegian border and as far south as Trelleborg on Sweden's southern tip. From Trelleborg, ferries connect the Swedish network with its German counterpart.

Stockholm is the only Swedish city with an underground rail system. The *T-banan*, as it is known, is very efficient and clean, and there are almost 100 stations covering 97 kilometres (60 miles) of track. The 'T' in *T-banan* stands for 'tunnel', and the letter can be found on signs at the entrances to underground stations. In Göteborg, a fleet of trams transports people around the city (see page 47).

Inlandsbanan

The most famous of Sweden's scenic railways is the *Inlandsbanan*, the Inland Railway, which connects the blue waters of the Öresund in the south with the snowy town of Gällivare, north of the Arctic Circle – a total distance of about 1300 km (800 miles).

The government first built the *Inlandsbanan* as a way of transporting the iron ore mined around Gällivare into southern Sweden. Today, the *Inlandsbanan* is no longer owned by the government but by the **municipalities** through which it passes. It still carries freight – some 32,000 containers' worth in 1995 – but it is also an important tourist attraction.

By road and air

In the 20th century, the government began a huge road-building programme. Sweden has 138,000 kilometres (85,750 miles) of road and most Swedish households own at least one car. Main roads connect all of Sweden's towns and cities, and motorways radiate from the most important of them – Stockholm, Göteborg and Malmö.

The sparsely populated central and northern regions have far fewer roads. Never-

The Öresund Link

The Öresund Link is one of the world's most ambitious engineering projects. Since the 19th century, there has been a succession of plans to provide a transportation link between the Swedish city of Malmö and the Danish capital, Copenhagen. The two cities are separated by only a 14-km-wide (9-mile) channel of water called the Öresund.

Work finally began on a cross-channel link in 1995. The Swedish and Danish governments agreed to build a road link that was part bridge and part tunnel. The 16-km-long (10-mile) link was completed on 14 August 1999 as the final section of the Öresund Bridge was placed in position. A few hours later, Crown Princess Victoria of Sweden and Crown Prince Frederik of Denmark met on the bridge to celebrate the event. The Öresund Link opened to traffic on 1 July 2000 – some nine years after the Danish and Swedish governments agreed to build the link in 1991. The picture above shows the bridge from the Swedish side. In the distance is an artificial island, built to take the road underground and on to Copenhagen.

theless, roads stretch along the Bothnian coast, connecting the string of settlements there, and to the very northern tip, far beyond the Arctic Circle.

Sweden's air transportation is largely controlled by the multinational Scandinavian Airlines System (SAS), which is jointly owned by the Swedish, Danish and Norwegian governments. SAS mainly operates international flights. Flights between Sweden's cities are run by another government-owned company called Linjeflyg. Stockholm alone has air connections to more than 30 other destinations in Sweden.

Arts and living

'... our land is big enough for the one who has a mind and spirit great enough to fill the empty expanses ...'

From *Gustav Adolf,* by 19th-century Swedish writer August Strindberg

The Swedes have an ancient tradition of giving and sharing. Although they love festivals and celebrations, Swedes adhere to an important principle that they express by the single word *lagom*, which means 'just enough'. The concept arose in Viking days, when people drank from a common bowl. It was understood without question that each person drank *lagom* – not too much but just enough – because he or she had to leave enough for others. Even today, Swedish society recognizes the importance of sharing and moderation – and not only in terms of food and drink.

Showy or excessive spending is not a trait the Swedes admire, and they are careful about how the way they live can affect not only the people around them but also their environment. The continuing relevance of the term *lagom* is nowhere clearer than in the great success of the Swedish **welfare state**, established after World War Two.

This principle of sharing also means that culture and the arts receive generous government funding. Grants given to theatres, opera houses and art galleries allow them to charge some of the lowest entrance fees and ticket prices in Europe. But funding is not restricted to the traditional arts – the idea of giving to all means that the government takes a very broad view of culture. Support is given to a range of projects, from restoring old Viking longboats to the building of traditional craft centres.

Despite the influence of more modern musical styles, folk dancing and folk music remain popular in Sweden, particularly during festivals.

FACT FILE

- The Vikings wrote using an ancient alphabet called the *futhark* (**runes**).

- The **Nobel Prize** for Literature has been awarded to Swedes six times. Only the United Kingdom, France and the USA have won the award more times.

- Swedes are avid readers. They spend an average of 30 minutes a day reading newspapers, and buy more books per person than any other European nation.

- The cost of living in Sweden is lower than it is in the United Kingdom. The UK is indexed at 99, while Sweden is indexed at 85.

ARTS FOR EVERYONE

The arts are part of everyday life in Sweden. The Swedish people are prepared to give a lot, through taxes and private donations, to preserve and enjoy their cultural heritage and to promote artistic creativity.

Everywhere in Sweden there are local, regional or nationally funded facilities, such as museums and theatres, designed to make the arts accessible to everyone. The National Travelling Theatre (*Riksteatern*) goes to cities and towns all over the country, and many visiting foreign companies, which perform mainly in Stockholm, also receive funding to travel to smaller towns.

Barrows, longhouses and cathedrals

These standing stones in the shape of a boat mark the burial site of an important warrior or leader. The boat shape shows the age-old importance attached to sailing in Swedish culture.

Throughout Sweden, there are buildings from every age of the country's long history. Some of the oldest surviving structures are barrows – huge burial mounds – that were built in the Bronze Age (1500–500 BC). Particularly impressive are the barrows on the island of Gotland. These feature enormous boulders arranged to look like boats (see below and page 20). Throughout southern Sweden, there are monuments of standing stones. At Smålandsstenar, there are five concentric circles of standing stones, which scholars believe formed a court of justice.

During Viking times, people lived, slept and ate together in long wooden halls known as longhouses. The longhouses were like upturned boats and were supported inside by two rows of pillars. The pillars of longhouses belonging to Viking leaders were richly carved and painted. Only fragments of these buildings survive today.

The longhouses provided the model for Sweden's first churches – called 'mast' churches because of the tall wooden pillars that held the roof up over the aisle. Soon, however, churches were built in the more impressive Gothic style that had first been developed in France and Germany. This was an age of great, soaring Gothic cathedrals, with luminous stained-glass windows and numerous sculptures of saints. In 1287, French architects travelled to Uppsala to rebuild the cathedral there.

The curved walls and roofs of the Viking longhouse made it look like an upturned boat. There were no windows and the roof was covered with thatch, wooden tiles or turf. Inside, the longhouse was divided into a large hall, with a hearth and vent to let out the smoke, a bedroom and a dairy.

Castles and cities

Starting in the 16th century, the Vasa kings and queens built lavish castles and palaces that were symbolic of their wealth and power. The royal palace of Drottningholm (see page 45) was modelled on the grandiose palace of the French kings at Versailles, near Paris. The architects built the palace in the elaborate style known as the Baroque.

In the 19th and 20th centuries, the authorities that governed Sweden's growing cities constructed buildings that expressed their civic and national pride. The Stockholm City Hall (Stadshuset) is one of the city's most imposing and beautiful buildings (see page 43). The building, completed in 1923, was constructed of some 8 million bricks and has a 137-metre-high (450-foot) tower. Inside is the Golden Hall, the walls of which are decorated with millions of golden mosaic tiles depicting scenes from Swedish history.

In the second quarter of the 20th century, many Swedish architects broke with traditional styles. The demand for new public buildings encouraged the construction of massive, unadorned buildings that used steel, concrete and other industrial materials. The leading architect of this modernist style was Gunnar Asplund (1885–1940).

Painting and sculpture

The Vikings were vigorous craftspeople. No object was too humble to be decorated. Expert smiths made bowls, platters and cups out of iron and copper and embellished them with scenes from myths and with intricate, interlocking patterns. Rarer gold and silver were made into shields and sword handles. Stonemasons made the hewn stones that still dot the Swedish landscape today. The stones often show Viking gods or commemorate battles and raids, and are sometimes inscribed with a runic alphabet (see box opposite).

Among Sweden's treasures from the medieval period are intricately carved baptismal fonts and splendid wood carvings. A number of wall paintings have survived, particularly in Gotland, Skåne and Östergötland. One of Sweden's most famous sculptures was carved by the German artist Bernt Notke (died 1509), who made the dramatic wooden statue of *Saint George and the Dragon* for Stockholm's cathedral (see page 41). The sculpture commemorates Sweden's victory over the Danes, which the Swedes attributed to the aid of the saint. The statue has many life-like details; the dragon's horns are real moose antlers.

This Viking rune-and-picture stone tells the story of a bloody family feud. Scholars think that the central figure in the box at the top is Odin, the most powerful of the Norse gods.

Some of Sweden's most famous painters lived at the end of the 19th century and the beginning of the 20th. A few of them formed a colony of *plein-air* artists at the village of Grez-sur-Loing in France. (*Plein air* – open air – is a

Runes and runestones

The Roman alphabet was only introduced to Sweden in the 11th century. Before then, the only form of writing was runes – a script that was first developed by the Germanic races of central Europe. Just as the Greek alphabet gets its name from its first two letters (*alpha* and *beta*), so the runic one gets its name from its first six letters (see above) – *futhark*.

The first runic alphabet had 24 letters, but by the Viking period, only sixteen were used (see above). Runes were thought to have magical properties, and the few people who could write them – the 'rune masters' – were regarded with suspicion and awe.

Runic messages were usually carved on tall standing stones, but some were carved on metal, bone or wood. The wooden ones are most often found in medieval churches. Runestones were placed beside frequently used paths, and they convey an enormous amount of information about everything from local people and buildings to great voyages.

Thousands of Swedish runestones have been found, most of them in Uppland around modern Uppsala. The most famous Swedish stone was found at Rök. It has 800 runes, and though scholars have been studying it for more than a century, it still has not been completely deciphered.

French term that refers to painting outdoors.) They included Carl Larsson (1853–1919), whose detailed depictions of everyday Swedish life are some of the most widely known and best-loved Swedish paintings. Another gifted painter of the time was Anders Zorn (1868–1920), whose work often depicted Swedish peasant life. The leading Swedish sculptor in the early 20th century was Carl Milles (1875–1955), who settled in the USA in 1931. Among his masterpieces is a monument to the Swedish hero Sten Sture near Uppsala.

The poets of
the Vikings were
known as *skalds*.
The legends and
tales that make
up Viking
literature are
called the Eddas.

Sagas and lays, novels and plays

Modern Swedish did not develop as a language until the 16th century, when the Bible was translated into Swedish for the first time. In Viking times, poets composed lays and sagas. Lays were epic poems recounting the adventures of the Norse gods and heroes. Sagas told stories from Viking history, such as the voyages to America or the foundation of Uppsala. They were not written down but passed on orally – that is, by word of mouth across the generations. Viking poetry was composed mostly in Icelandic but is part of the shared heritage of all **Scandinavian** countries.

The first golden age of Swedish literature came in the 17th century, when the country was beginning to assert itself as a powerful European nation. Scholars translated the Viking sagas, while poets such as Georg Stiernhielm (1598–1672) wrote long, stirring poems that glorified the nation. Others wrote gentle love poems or rousing drinking songs. Writers wanted to show that Swedish was a vigorous and adaptable language. They wanted to create a literature that could rival the more established ones of France, Italy and England.

In the 18th century, poetry and drama flourished under the patronage of King Gustav III (reigned 1771–92). The two outstanding writers of the period, however, were not poets or dramatists but scientists. Carl von Linné (see page 36), usually known as Linnaeus, wrote his massive *Species Plantarum*, and Emanuel Swedenborg (1688–1772) not only edited the first Swedish scientific periodical but also wrote religious meditations.

In the 19th century, many different kinds of writing flourished. Some authors wrote imaginative retellings of old Norse stories, while others strove to give truthful depictions of contemporary Swedish life.

A love poem

This short, simple love poem, entitled 'Love Me', was written by Maria Wine (born 1912), one of Sweden's most famous modern poets.

Love me
but do not come too near
leave room for love
to laugh at happiness
always let some of my blond
hair be free.

August Strindberg

August Strindberg is Sweden's most brilliant and influential writer. He was born in Stockholm in 1849 and began his writing career as a struggling journalist. His first play, *Mäster Olaf*, was rejected by the Royal Theatre. Undaunted, Strindberg went on to write numerous novels, short stories and plays, in which he set out to portray contemporary Swedish life.

Theatre audiences who were used to wordy tragedies and laboured comedies were astonished by the realism and intensity of his plays, such as *The Father* and *Miss Julie*. The dialogue was sharp and colloquial and the plots dramatic and tense. Their subject matter dealt with some of the most fiercely debated issues of the time, such as women's rights and mental illness.

Strindberg was highly emotional and had two unhappy marriages. Later in life, he suffered a mental breakdown and became deeply religious. His last plays, such as *The Dance of Death,* are dream-like and full of the playwright's rather gloomy ideas about sin and punishment. Strindberg's intensity can also be felt in his dramatic paintings of Sweden's landscapes (above).

Emile Flygare-Carlén, for example, wrote moving stories about life in the villages of Sweden's west coast. The towering literary figure of the 19th century, however, is the playwright August Strindberg (see box).

Several Swedes have won the Nobel Prize for Literature, but only two of these have achieved an international reputation. Selma Lagerlöf (1858–1940), who wrote for both adults and children, won the prize in 1909. In 1951, Pär Lagerkvist (1891–1974), a novelist, poet and playwright, won the prize for his novel *Barabbas.* Another much loved Swedish children's author

The fiddler

At the heart of Swedish folk music is the fiddle (folk violin). Fiddlers – *spelman* – played at village dances and ceremonies and passed on their melodies by example rather than in the form of written music. Only rarely could a rural fiddler read music and there was a great deal of improvisation.

At the end of the 19th century, preachers denounced the fiddle as the 'devil's instrument'. Many fiddlers stopped playing, and some even smashed their instruments. One of Sweden's most famous fiddlers, Hjort Anders (1865–1952), however, was determined to keep playing. He would step unexpectedly into a village church and play a particularly wild tune called the 'Devil's Polka'.

More recently, there has been a revival of fiddle playing. Villages have their own ensembles and old melodies are being collected and revived.

One of Sweden's best-loved singers, Evert Taube, is remembered in this lively statue in Stockholm's Gamla Stan.

is Astrid Lindgren. First published in the 1940s, her Pippi Longstocking books have been translated into over 50 languages and made into films and TV programmes. The Swedes call Lindgren Tant Astrid (Aunt Astrid) and regard her as a national treasure.

Making music

Swedish people love to sing. Swedes often make up their own songs to celebrate special occasions, such as weddings and birthdays. A popular hobby among Swedes is singing in choirs. In the 19th century, one of the most famous singers in the world was the Swedish soprano Jenny Lind (1820–87), known as 'the Swedish Nightingale'. Her picture appears on the Swedish 50-*krona* note (see page 8).

A great variety of folk dancing and folk music can still be seen and heard all over Sweden – each region has its own favourites. In the mountains, peasant women sang or played simple melodies as a way of herding the animals in their care. They used a long birchwood trumpet called a *lur* or sang in a very high-pitched voice. Their voices could carry as far as 5 kilometres (3 miles) away. These beautiful old herding melodies are today being revived.

Popular folk instruments include the fiddle, accordion and the *nyckelharpa*. The *nyckelharpa* player sits with the instrument

across his or her lap and bows it like a violin. Instead of changing the notes by pressing on the strings with the fingers, the player holds down keys. Today, the *nyckelharpa* is particularly popular in Uppsala county. In the late 19th century, folk music inspired several distinguished Swedish composers, including Wilhelm Peterson-Berger and Hugo Alfvén.

Sweden also has a lively pop music scene. One of the most successful groups ever, Abba, shot to world fame after winning the Eurovision Song Contest in 1974. More recent international stars have included Ace of Base, Roxette, the Cardigans and Inner Circle, all of whom perform and record in English.

Directors and actors

Sweden has a small but well-respected film industry. The most famous Swedish film director is Ingmar Bergman (born 1918), who has made masterpieces such as *Wild Strawberries* (1957) and *Fanny and Alexander* (1982), a magical tale about family life in Uppsala at

With such songs as 'Waterloo' and 'Mamma Mia', Swedish band Abba helped define the pop culture of the 1970s.

Traditional Sami handicrafts, such as these pieces of embroidery, are sold at fairs all over the far north of Sweden.

the end of the 19th century. Perhaps the Swedes best known abroad are the actresses Ingrid Bergman (1915–82) and Greta Garbo (1905–90). Bergman won Oscars for her roles in *Gaslight* (1943), *Anastasia* (1956) and *Murder on the Orient Express* (1974). Garbo, who lived as a recluse for most of her life, made her mark in the 1930s with films such as *Anna Karenina* (1935) and *Camille* (1936). In 1933, she played Sweden's famous Queen Christina.

More recently, the Swedish director Lasse Hallström gained recognition for his award-winning films *My Life as a Dog* (1985) – about a young boy living with relatives in the Swedish countryside in the 1950s – and the popular *What's Eating Gilbert Grape?* (1993), made in the USA. Mai Zetterling is still known abroad mainly for her fine acting performances in numerous films from Sweden, France and Hollywood. Today, Zetterling also works as a director.

Keeping the past alive

Red-painted wooden horses – called dalahästar – are made in Sweden's beautiful Dalarna region. The horses were first made by two brothers in 1928. Today, the horses are almost a national symbol.

The Swedes' close relationship with the land is reflected in their vibrant folk culture. Country crafts such as wood-carving, weaving and glass-blowing (see page 86) are flourishing industries. Especially popular are boots and rucksacks made from *näver* – the inner bark of the birch tree. After being cut into strips and left to cure, it resembles soft leather.

The Jokkmokk Fair

Every February, the **Sami** town of Jokkmokk in Sweden's far north holds a big crafts fair that attracts visitors from all over the country. The fair has been held in the town since 1605. The Sami have traditionally used the **natural resources** they found around them to make their crafts: elaborate knife handles carved from reindeer horn, baskets woven from roots and beautiful textiles with simple, colourful designs (see opposite). The stall owners wear the Sami folk costume – warm fur garments and hats that are trimmed with red and yellow embroidery and ribbons (see page 30).

The highlight of the fair is the reindeer race (above) that takes place on a frozen lake. People gather on the shoreline, drinking black coffee flavoured with salt and singing light-hearted songs called *joiks*. They have to keep an eye on the race, though, as sometimes the racing reindeer can slip and skid into the crowd.

Folk music and dancing are very popular, too. Most towns have folk dance clubs and bands of folk musicians. Fiddlers in traditional costume can be found at almost every festival. In village bars, musicians often while away the time by playing a tune or two.

On special occasions, people still wear the colourful national costume with pride. For men, this consists of embroidered waistcoats, breeches and felt hats. Women wear flared skirts, brightly coloured aprons and waist-coats, and white bonnets. The clothes are often embroidered with beautiful floral designs. Sweden's queen, Silvia, wears the national costume on public occasions, such as the king's birthday and National Day.

Children learn traditional handicrafts in school so that the skills will not be lost. Knitting, embroidery and woodcarving, along with the less well-known crafts of lacemaking, rug-making, candle-making and even black-smithing are still enjoyed as hobbies by young and old.

Swedish homes are usually well designed and well equipped.

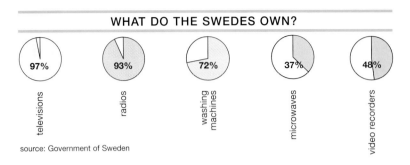

WHAT DO THE SWEDES OWN?

97%	93%	72%	37%	48%
televisions	radios	washing machines	microwaves	video recorders

source: Government of Sweden

EVERYDAY LIFE

Most Swedes today live in towns and cities. Only a hundred years ago, however, the vast majority lived in the countryside. Many people today still feel a strong connection to the land. They may have relations who live on a farm or in a village and spend their holidays there. Or their grandparents may tell them stories about growing up on a farm and pass on some of the old rural traditions and folklore.

Most Swedish households still consist of parents and their children. Most couples have just one or two children. Today, though, unmarried couples with children are almost as common as married ones. Under Swedish law, all couples, whether married or unmarried, have the same rights. Increasingly, too, children are brought up by a single parent, usually the mother. The divorce rate in Sweden is higher than in some other European countries, but not as high as the UK divorce rate.

Young people rarely live at home while they attend university, and some live on their own between the ages of sixteen and nineteen while they finish their last two or three years of schooling.

HOW SWEDES SPEND THEIR MONEY

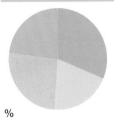

%

31.4 housing and energy

19.8 food

16.1 transportation

9.8 education and recreation

22.9 other

source: Government of Sweden

The Swedes are home lovers and spend a lot of their income on housing and food.

Supporting families

Children do not begin school until they are at least six years old, but most toddlers go to a day-care centre (see page 87) or nursery school, or are entrusted to the care of a *dagmamma*, a 'mother-for-the-day' (child-minder). Most Swedish parents – both men and women – go out to work, so, after the age of eighteen months, children usually attend playgroup so they can socialize and learn to make friends.

The playgroups – or dayhomes (*daghem* or *dagis* for short), as they are called in Sweden – are provided by the local authorities. They were first set up in the 1930s in order to give all adults – both rich and poor – a chance to have a career. Parents pay about 10 or 15 per cent of the costs; the rest is met by local taxes. At the end of the day, some children go to *fritids* (after-school care) until their parents can pick them up after work.

All parents are entitled to take time off from work – up to one year's paid leave – to look after a new baby. The parents can choose to split the twelve months between them in whatever way they wish, but at least one month must be taken by the father. Paid leave is also allowed to parents whose child is ill, even after the child starts school.

Living space

Whether they live in the city or in the countryside, nearly all Swedes live in well-equipped, spacious homes. During the 20th century, the government built or helped

Traditional Swedish houses are made of wood and painted in bright colours.

to build hundreds of thousands of new homes. More than half of Sweden's current houses and apartments were built after 1960. Apartments are often just as spacious and well designed as houses. Swedish homes everywhere are usually simply and elegantly furnished and full of light.

At weekends or during holidays, Swedes who live in towns and cities like to go and relax in the countryside. In 1998, there were more than 600,000 holiday homes in Sweden. Many of them are recently built seaside or lakeside cottages, often within easy travelling distance of big cities such as Stockholm and Göteborg.

Some city dwellers renovate old abandoned farmhouses and small farms to use as country homes. Building near lakes or beaches or on forest land is strictly regulated to ensure that these valuable natural areas do not become overcrowded or inaccessible to walkers. Given the number of lakes in Sweden, it is not surprising that one in every five households in Sweden also owns a boat.

Smörgåsbord

The famous Swedish *smörgåsbord* is an enormous buffet that includes a whole range of dishes. The buffet was originally served as a kind of appetizer to a festive meal. Guests could snack on herrings, bread and cheese before sitting down to the main meal. The word *'smörgås'* means simply a 'slice of bread', while *'bord'* means 'table'.

Today, the *smörgåsbord* is still reserved for special occasions. It includes not only slices of herring, served with horseradish or mustard, but also *gravadlax* (thinly sliced salmon cured in dill), meatballs, open sandwiches and sometimes smoked reindeer.

'Tack för maten'

The standard family meal in Sweden consists of sausages, potatoes and possibly some other root vegetables. Soups are also very popular. Swedish families often eat soup on Tuesdays or Thursdays, depending on regional or family custom. Table manners are very formal, and children are taught to say *'Tack för maten'* – 'Thank you for the food' – after finishing their meal, especially if they are eating at a friend's or relative's house.

Semlor

In the Christian calendar, Lent is the six weeks that lead up to Easter. During this time, bakeries in Sweden are full of Lenten buns (*semlor*), bread rolls full of marzipan and cream. These delicious buns are especially popular with children and are easy to make at home.

You will need:
6 soft, round white bread rolls
icing sugar
70 g (2½ oz) marzipan or almond paste
125 ml (4 fl oz) double cream
cinnamon

Method:
Carefully cut a small section off the top of each roll and put it aside. With a teaspoon, dig a hollow in the base of each roll. On a work surface dusted with icing sugar, knead the marzipan until soft. Cut it into six pieces and shape each piece to fit the hollow. Whip the cream until soft peaks form. Put a big spoonful of cream into each roll on top of the marzipan. Replace the tops of the rolls. Dust with icing sugar and cinnamon to add sweetness.

Swedes also like to eat out in restaurants quite often. A traditional *dagens rätt* (daily special) served in a restaurant might consist of *pyttipanna*, a dish of minced beef and potato topped with a fried egg (similar to corned-beef hash), or *Janssons frestelse*, a dish of cheese, potatoes and anchovies.

Fish has been an important part of the Swedish diet from earliest times. Herring used to be a staple, but overfishing and pollution have meant that most fish are no longer cheap enough to be considered everyday food. Even so, fish comes in many varieties – pickled, smoked or fresh – and the different ways in which herring and salmon are served are too numerous even to list. Swedish delicacies now include lobster and the *löjrom* of Norrland, a pinkish caviar that comes from a species of Baltic herring.

The Swedes love to eat herrings so much that there is a *smörgåsbord* that consists only of herring dishes – the *sillbricka*.

college
and university   31%

secondary   98%
school

primary   100%
school

*Swedes think of
education as
something that
should be pursued
throughout life.
About one-third
of Swedes study
at university level,
with many adults
returning to college
later in life to gain
further education.*

Education: a basic right

Children begin school at six or seven, and they must attend full-time education for nine years. An average class has only 22 pupils, and during the first six years, each class has one teacher for most subjects. In secondary schools, different subjects are taught by different teachers, as in the United Kingdom.

Certain subjects are compulsory: Swedish, English, maths, social studies (including geography, history and religion), science (including biology, chemistry and physics) and physical education. In addition, both boys and girls usually study home economics and crafts, such as sewing and woodworking. There are many elective subjects, and students often choose to study other languages in addition to the compulsory English. German is the most popular choice.

Only 1.1 per cent of all school-aged children in Sweden are enrolled in private schools; all the rest attend government-funded schools. Home schooling is not allowed. Children may leave school after they have completed the compulsory nine years, usually at age sixteen, but few do. The vast majority stay on for two or three more years to get either vocational training or to qualify for admission to higher education.

During the last two to three years, students specialize in selected areas. They are allowed to choose from sixteen different national study programmes, or they can create their own individually tailored programme. They are similar to A-level courses in the United Kingdom.

Slightly more than 30 per cent of the Swedish workforce are educated beyond the typical eleven to twelve years. However, the number is increasing as the demand for skilled workers grows. The largest expansion is occurring at small and medium-sized colleges, which specialize in vocational training.

Sweden is one of the biggest spenders in the world on education, allocating 8.3 per cent of its **gross national product** (GNP) on education in 1999.

Many students take part in after-school activities, such as sports, guides and scouts, piano lessons and extra study. The state offers funding for childcare and also for *fritids*, where children of working parents are looked after until their parents return from work in the evening. There, the children can learn new hobbies, sometimes study another language or receive extra tutoring in certain subjects.

How to say ...

Sweden's official language is Swedish (*svenska*), the mother tongue of the vast majority of its citizens. Swedish belongs to the Germanic family of languages, which also includes Danish, Dutch, German and English. This means that a few words look and sound quite similar to words in English with the same meaning – for example, *båt* ('boat'), *bok* ('book') and *strand* ('strand', meaning 'beach').
In addition to Swedish, there are two minority languages – Sami and Finnish.

Although it is related to English, Swedish is a difficult language to learn. Not only are some of its individual sounds difficult to say correctly, but also, when spoken, it has a sing-song quality that takes a long time to reproduce. However, it is not hard to find English speakers in Sweden, especially in the cities, because all Swedes learn English at school. When visiting any country, it is an advantage to be able to speak at least a few words in the language – even if only to apologize for not being able to speak more! Most Swedes are exceptionally polite, and expect visitors to behave with good manners. Here are a few phrases in Swedish:

Thank you   *Tack* (tak)

Yes   *Ja* (yah)

No   *Nej* (neh)

Hello   *Hej* (heh)

Good morning   *God morgon* (god morgon)

Good afternoon   *God middag* (god middag)

Good night   *God natt* (God natt)

Sorry   *Förlåt* (ferrlot)

Excuse me   *Ursäkta* (ursawktah)

I don't understand   *Jag föstår inte* (yag ferstor inte)

Do you speak English?   *Talar du engelska* (talar doo enyelska)

I am English   *Jag är engelsk* (yag ehr enyelsk)

What is your name?   *Vad heter du?* (vad heter doo)

What is this called in Swedish?   *Vad heter det här på svenska?* (vad heter det hor peh svenska)

Sports: out in the fresh air

In Sweden, every town or local area has its own recreation committee, which ensures everyone can enjoy exercise and the great outdoors. The Swedish Sports Confederation reckons that some 500,000 Swedes belong to a sports club, of which there are over 22,000 in the country. The confederation also estimates that more than 66 per cent of boys and 55 per cent of girls between the ages of seven and fifteen belong to a sports club.

Football is a popular sport in Sweden. The national team, which wears the blue and yellow of Sweden's flag, usually does well in international competitions.

Tennis

Sweden is one of the world's most successful tennis nations. It is estimated that there are some 400,000 regular players of the game in Sweden – out of a total population of less than 9 million – and more than 25% of these players are under fourteen.

There are lots of tennis tournaments, too. The two biggest are the Båstad Open, held in late summer, and the Stockholm Open, held in autumn. Thousands of people come to watch the tournaments. The show court at Stockholm, housed in a huge dome to the south of the city, seats up to 16,000 spectators. The Donald Duck Cup is the biggest junior tournament in the country – thousands of children take part every year.

The popularity of tennis in Sweden today is largely the work of Sweden's most famous tennis star, Björn Borg (below). His brilliant example has inspired generations of young tennis players, including Stefan Edberg and Magnus Gustafsson. Borg won the Donald Duck Cup at the age of fifteen and was only sixteen when he made his tennis debut for Sweden's Davis Cup team. In 1974, before the age of nineteen, Borg captured nine tournament titles, including his first French Open. By the time he retired, aged 26, in 1983, he had won 62 men's singles titles and four doubles titles.

Other popular sports are tennis, surfing, swimming, golf, skiing and running. As might be expected in a country with such beautiful mountains, forests and lakes, walking and cycling attract many thousands of enthusiasts in Sweden.

Religion

Some 90 per cent of Sweden's population belong to the **Lutheran Church** of Sweden, the national Protestant church that broke away from the Roman Catholic Church some 500 years ago. Only about 5 per cent of Swedes attend church regularly, however. As in other Western countries, many Christians attend church only at Christmas and Easter and for special ceremonies. Most children are baptized, for example, and most weddings and funerals take place in church. Many Swedish children choose to be confirmed – that is, accepted as a member of the church – at fourteen and go to a 'confirmation camp' to prepare.

Since the 1940s, **immigrants** from all over the world have brought their own religions with them. Stockholm alone now has at least three Muslim mosques, at least one Greek Orthodox church and several synagogues, as well as Lutheran churches. There is also a growing number of Pentecostal churches in Sweden.

Good health

Sweden is one of the healthiest nations in the world. Life expectancy is very high: 78 years for men and 83 for women. All Swedish residents are covered by national health insurance. People aged under nineteen receive free health care, dental treatment and eye check-ups. The government also subsidizes the cost of spectacles. Adults have to pay for these things, but not the full price. Children in Sweden enjoy a very high standard of general health, and the population as a whole has been getting healthier with each generation since the 1930s.

Nevertheless, in recent years, concerns about high levels of government spending have led to some drastic cutbacks in health care. Today, the Swedish government spends about 8 per cent of its gross national product (GNP) on health care – more than the UK spends but less than Germany and France.

Despite the cutbacks, though, Sweden's medical provision is among the world's best. Anyone registered in the Swedish social system can receive emergency health care at any hospital, similar to the system in the UK.

Festivals and celebrations

Swedes love to celebrate. Traditionally a people of the countryside, they continue to mark the passing of the seasons with lively festivals. Music and dance often play an important role. City dwellers keep old country customs, and even today people like to dress in folk costume on special occasions. Many of the celebrations that occur throughout the year in Sweden are held on holy days. Though some retain religious significance, most have become secular festivals – holidays to be enjoyed by all.

After the long winter months, Swedes look forward to Easter, which, besides being an important Christian festival, marks the beginning of spring. During Lent, they eat *semlor* (see page 109) and homes are decorated with *påskris*, birch twigs with coloured feathers attached to the ends. The twigs are not only a sign of new life but also a reminder of the flagellation (whipping) of Christ before he died.

On the Thursday before Easter Eve (*Skärtorsdag*), girls dress up as witches and go around the district asking for treats such as sweets or small change. An old Swedish legend tells how, on the day before Christ was crucified, witches flew on broomsticks to meet the Devil. In some places, people set off fireworks and light bonfires to scare off the witches.

Midsummer (*Midsommar*) is one of Sweden's most popular festivals, celebrated on the weekend that falls closest to 24 June – the Feast of Saint John the Baptist. In northern parts of Sweden, the sun barely sets at all on this day, and everywhere people enjoy the long daylight hours. A maypole wreathed in wildflowers and birch twigs is set up for people to dance around. The festival has its origins in pagan sun worship.

National holidays

Sweden has thirteen public holidays. These are usually times of celebration rather than relaxation.

1 January	New Year's Day
6 January	Epiphany
March/April	Good Friday
	Easter Monday
1 May	Labour Day/
	Ascension Day
May	Whit Sunday
21 June	Midsummer Eve
22 June	Midsummer Day
2 November	All Saints' Day
24 December	Christmas Eve
25 December	Christmas Day
26 December	Boxing Day
31 December	New Year's Eve

Christmas lasts a long time in Sweden. Celebrations begin just after Saint Lucia's Day (13 December) and last until January, when the decorations are taken down. Saint Lucia's Day is named in honour of a Sicilian saint whose name means 'light'. Traditionally, the oldest girl in the family dressed in a white robe tied with a red sash and wore electric 'candles' in her hair. Today, schoolchildren sing songs dedicated to Lucia.

Christmas is celebrated with feasting. The Christmas meal is on 24 December. The traditional dishes are ham and a type of fish called *lutfisk*, with rice pudding for dessert. After the meal come presents. One of the family dresses up as the Christmas gnome, or *jultomten*, who knocks on the door and hands out presents. The festival called Knut, on 13 January, marks the end of Christmas.

National Day

Since 1916, the Swedes have celebrated 6 June as Swedish Flag Day. Since 1983, however, this has been called *Nationaldag* (National Day). It is a day of national pride and celebration. The day marks the anniversary of the day in 1523 when the first truly Swedish king, Gustav Vasa, was chosen to rule, and the day in 1809 when a new Swedish **constitution** was signed.

On National Day, the king and queen attend a ceremony held at Skansen, at which they present flags to the various trade guilds. Everywhere there are parades and celebrations. Many Swedish homes have flagpoles from which they fly the flag. However, unlike the national days of many other countries, the day is not a holiday.

During Sweden's Midsommar festival, people dance around a maypole and feast long into the night.

The future

'... people want more justice, more fairness and more money spent on the public sector.'

Social Democratic Party secretary, Ingela Thaler

If Swedes living in the 19th century could visit Sweden today, they would be amazed at the transformation their country has undergone. In the 19th century, Sweden was among the poorest nations in Europe. The majority of people lived and worked in the countryside. Most children lived in poverty, and wealth was largely in the hands of a privileged few. Today, Sweden can boast one of the fairest societies in the world, where the government works hard to make sure that everyone has *lagom* – 'just enough'. Despite the achievements of the 20th century, Sweden faces a number of problems that must be solved if its citizens are to preserve the privileges and high living standards they have enjoyed for more than fifty years.

SAVING JOBS

Many Swedes today are worried about unemployment. Like many other Western countries, Sweden is moving from an industry-based to a service-based economy. Whereas industry provided mass employment, service industries, such as banking and tourism, require fewer but more highly skilled workers.

Since the 1990s, the government and private companies have worked hard to make sure that the country's industrial base is not lost. In order to make more goods to sell abroad, industry needs to expand by improving productivity, and then slowly increasing the number of

In the late 20th century, great industrial cities such as Malmö and Göteborg went into decline as they struggled to compete in a fierce world market.

FACT FILE

● Swedes remain uncertain about closer ties with Europe. After voting to join the European Union in 1995 by only a 5% margin, they have – along with the UK and Denmark – yet to join the European single currency, the euro.

● Sweden has one of the highest rates of Internet use in the world. There are 86 Internet hosts per 100 people, compared with 39 per 100 in the UK.

● In January 2000, Stockholm hosted a three-day forum on the Holocaust, which ended with a commitment by 46 countries to keep alive the memory of the victims of the Nazi genocide.

employees without raising costs. The government's and businesses' efforts seem to be working. The volume and value of Swedish **exports** have grown substantially and industrial profits have increased. By the late 1990s, the latter had exceeded the high records achieved in the 1980s.

Some economic uncertainty lingers, however. The instability of many national economies, including Japan and Russia, at the turn of the new millennium still threatens the global markets. Sweden could be particularly vulnerable in a worldwide slowdown because its prosperity is so dependent on exports. Many Swedes, too, are uneasy about the power of multinational companies. If they continue to work cooperatively with the government, as they have in the recent past, then there may be no problem.

Racism

In the early 1990s, along with high unemployment, Sweden experienced racist attacks against some of its immigrant groups for the first time. As in several other European countries, including France and Germany, right-wing neo-Nazi groups are on the rise. Only a tiny number of Swedes are involved, however. Most Swedes are passionately against racism. Since the economy started to improve, however, there has been no recurrence of racial violence.

THE ENVIRONMENT

The Swedish people have voted to phase out the production of nuclear energy by 2010. However, 43 per cent of the country's energy comes from its nuclear power plants. Sweden does not have its own resources of coal or oil, so the government will either have to **import** huge amounts of fuel or find a way to replace the energy domestically. Whatever solution is found, filling the gap left by the nuclear power plants will be expensive.

Young Swedes regard the environment as one of the two most pressing political issues facing Sweden; the other is employment. Indeed, because the countryside and wildlife are so important to Swedes, they have sometimes outshone other countries in their attempts to protect the environment. For instance, the percentage of paper that Sweden recycles is one of the highest in Europe. But there is still much to do. Demand for energy is still very high, and careless exploitation of the country's timber and **hydroelectric** resources have in the past caused environmental damage. Sustainability – the use of the Earth's resources without damaging its ability to renew itself – is an increasingly vital goal for Sweden, as it is for the rest of the world.

21ST-CENTURY ISSUES

The Swedes' relationship with the **European Union** (EU) continues to be double-edged. Swedes voted to join the EU by only the narrowest of majorities, and they decided not to participate in the European Monetary Union (EMU) when it came into use in 1999.

Many Swedes, it seems, are having second thoughts about membership in the EU. However, they recognize that Sweden's future prosperity depends on closer relationships with its European neighbours. Since Viking times, Sweden has been an outward-looking nation. The Öresund Link between Sweden and Denmark is symbolic of the fact that this attitude is still alive.

European Monetary Union

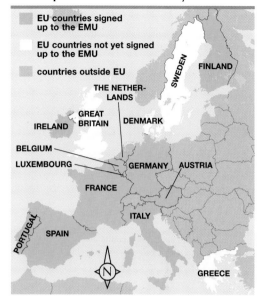

EU countries signed up to the EMU

EU countries not yet signed up to the EMU

countries outside EU

The map above shows those countries of the European Union (EU) that joined the European Monetary Union (EMU) in 1999. Greece joined later, in 2001.

A BRIGHT FUTURE?

The future looks promising for Sweden. The owner of one of the country's largest companies once said that Sweden had learnt a valuable lesson: if you want to improve your child's standard of living, you have to make sure that everyone else's child also has a better quality of life, too. Although it may be impossible to raise everyone's standard of living to the same high degree, the continued search to improve life for everyone should mean that Sweden will forge ahead in the 21st century.

Sweden's future is closely bound to that of the European Union, whose flag is shown below.

Almanac

POLITICAL

country name:
official form: Kingdom of
    Sweden
short form: Sweden
local official form: Konungariket
    Sverige
local short form: Sverige

nationality:
    noun: Swede
    adjective: Swedish

official language: Swedish

capital city:
    Stockholm

type of government:
    constitutional monarchy

suffrage (voting rights):
    everyone eighteen years and over

national anthem: 'Du gamla, du fria'

national holiday:
    6 June (National Day)

flag:

GEOGRAPHICAL

location: northern Europe

climate: temperate in the south;
    subarctic in the north

total area: 450,000 sq km
    (174,000 sq miles)
    land: 91%
    water: 9%

coastline: 7564 km (4700 miles)

terrain: mostly flat lowlands;
    mountains in the west

highest point: Kebnekaise,
    2123 m (6965 ft)
lowest point: Baltic Sea coast
    0 m

land use:
    forests and woodland: 68%
    arable land: 7%
    permanent pastures: 1%
    other: 24%

natural resources: timber, iron, copper,
    silver, lead, zinc, uranium

natural hazards: ice floes in
    surrounding waters

POPULATION

population (2000): 8.9 million

average population density (2000):
22 people per sq km (57 people per sq mile)

urban population:
83%

population growth rate (2000):
0.03%

birth rate (2000): 8.2 births per 1000 of the population

death rate (2000): 10.6 deaths per 1000 of the population

sex ratio (2000):
98 males per 100 females

total fertility rate (2000):
1.5 children per woman

infant mortality rate (2000):
3.4 deaths per 1000 live births

life expectancy at birth (2000):
total population: 79 years
male: 78 years
female: 83 years

literacy:
total population: 99%

ECONOMY

currency: Swedish *krona* (SKr);
1 SKr = 100 *öre*

exchange rate (2002):
£1 = SKr 14.38

gross national product (2000):
£149,187 million

gross national product by sectors:
agriculture: 2.2%
industry: 30.5%
services: 67.3%

GNP per capita (2000): £16,844

average annual growth rate (1990–99):
1.6%

average annual inflation rate
(1990–2000): 2.3%

unemployment rate (1999): 5.6%

exports (2000): £52,937 million
imports (2000): £42,750 million

foreign aid given (2000): £1019 million

Human Development Index
(an index scaled from 0 to 100 combining statistics indicating adult literacy, years of schooling, life expectancy, and income levels):
92.6 (UK 91.8)

TIMELINE – SWEDEN

World history

Swedish history

c.15,000 BC

c.8000 The city of Jericho is founded

c.15,000 Ice covers Sweden

c.6000 Humans inhabit Sweden

c.1500 BC

753 Traditional date of the foundation of Rome

492–479 Wars between Persia and Greek city-states

c.1500 Swedish trade routes reach as far as central Europe

c.AD 150 Tacitus describes the Svears of central Sweden

c.AD 300

306 Constantine becomes Roman emperor and legalizes Christianity

c.1000 Vikings land in North America

c.800–1000 Viking traders and warriors expand through northern Europe

829 Saint Ansgar brings Christianity to Sweden

c.1000 Sweden begins to unite

1689 Peter I becomes tsar of Russia

1642–51 The English Civil War

1618 Thiry Years' War breaks out

1520 Birth of Protestantism – the pope expels Martin Luther from the Roman Catholic Church

1492 Columbus lands in America

1453 Turks capture Constantinople

1445 Gutenberg prints the first European book

1348 Black Death breaks out in Europe

1066 The Normans conquer Britain

1630 Gustavus Adolph enters the Thirty Years' War

1560–1658 Sweden's kings and queens build a Baltic empire

1544 Swedish Crown becomes hereditary

1520s The birth of Protestantism in Sweden

1523 Gustav founds the Vasa dynasty

c.1500

1415 Sweden completes the conquest of Finland

1397 Margaret proclaims the Union of Kalmar between Sweden, Denmark and Norway

1160–1250 The Sverkers and Eriks contend the throne

c.1100

c.1700

1738 The first spinning machine is patented in England

1751–72 Publication in France of the *Encyclopedia* – a key work in the Enlightenment

1789 The French Revolution breaks out

1700–21 Defeat in the Great Northern War leaves Sweden ruling only Sweden and Finland

1735 Linnaeus publishes the *Systema Naturae*

1792 Gustav III is assassinated

2000 The West celebrates the Millennium – 2000 years since the birth of Christ

2000 The Örseund Link is opened, joining Malmö and Copenhagen

c.2000

1999 Sweden decides not to join the European single currency – the euro

1995 Sweden joins the European Union (EU)

1986 Prime Minister Olaf Palme is assassinated

c.1800

1804 Napoleon crowns himself emperor of France

1815 Napoleon is defeated at Waterloo

1848 Famine prompts unrest in much of Europe

1853–6 The Crimean War

1871 Bismarck unites German states into a single country

1810 Napoleon's marshal Bernadotte becomes Crown Prince of Sweden

1814 Sweden forces Norway into a union that lasts until 1905

1866 The personal power of the monarch ends

1867–8 Famine forces Swedish migration to the USA, among other countries

1989 Communism collapses in eastern Europe

1979 Former Soviet Union invades Afghanistan

1973 World oil crisis

c. 1970

1945–60 Swedish welfare state is created

1932 Social Democrats become governing party

1921 Women receive the vote

1901 First Nobel prizes awarded

1939–45 World War Two

1933 Adolf Hitler becomes German chancellor

1914–18 World War One

c.1900

Glossary

abdication formal relinquishing of power by a ruler of a country

Allemansrätt (Sw. 'the Right of Common Access') unwritten Swedish law that allows access to any land provided no damage is caused

archipelago chain of islands

biodiversity variety of wildlife in a habitat

capitalism economic and political system based on trade and on individuals' accumulation of wealth and property – that is, capital

coalition sharing of government between two or more political parties

coat of arms emblem of a nation or family. The design is usually made up of symbolic objects such as crowns.

colony overseas territory settled by another country

coniferous plants or trees that keep their leaves in the winter; sometimes known as evergreens

constitution fundamental principles that underlie the government of a country

constitutional monarchy monarchy that rules according to a constitution

democracy process that allows the people of a country to govern themselves, usually by voting for a leader or leaders

empire extent of overseas territories owned or ruled by a country

euro unit of the single European currency

European Union (EU) organization made up of European countries that work together on many economic, social and political issues

exports goods sold by one country to another

glacier large, permanent mass of ice that forms over thousands of years

gross national product (GNP) total value of goods and services produced by a country during a period, usually a year

hydroelectricity electricity produced by harnessing the water power of rivers

immigration arrival and settlement in a country of people from overseas, known as immigrants

imports goods bought by one country from another

industrialized nation country where manufacture is usually carried out with the help of machinery

investment lending of money to businesses and organizations to allow growth and expansion

lagom (Sw. 'just enough') Swedish principle of sharing and moderation

län (Sw.) Swedish county headed by a governor

Lutheran Church Christian denomination that follows the teachings of the father of Protestantism, Martin Luther (1483–1546)

migration movement of individuals or groups from one place to another

missionary member of a religious mission. Missions aim to teach and convert people to a particular religion.

monarchy form of government in which a monarch – king or queen – is head of state

municipality administrative subdivision of a *län*

national debt money owed by a nation because of loans made to it

natural resources products and features of the Earth that support life or satisfy people's needs

neutrality policy of not becoming involved in disputes between other nations

Nobel prizes awards in the sciences, arts and politics founded by the Swedish manufacturer Alfred Nobel (1833–96)

nomadic describes a lifestyle that involves migration from place to place in search of food or shelter

peninsula finger of land stretching out into a sea or lake

prehistory time before written or recorded history

Reformation religious movement in the 16th century that led to the formation of Protestantism

runes script used in Sweden before the 11th century

Sami earliest native inhabitants of Scandinavia

Scandinavia collective name often used for the countries of Norway, Sweden, Denmark and Iceland

socialism political theory that teaches that society as a whole should be in control of a country's resources and businesses

thing Viking assembly that decided on the law for a community

treeline altitude above which no trees will grow

tundra treeless marshland in the north of Sweden

welfare state social system where the government is responsible for the well-being of its citizens

Bibliography

Major sources used for this book
Parker, Geoffrey, and S. Adams (eds), *The Thirty Years' War* (Routledge Kegan & Paul, 1997)
Svenska Institutet, *Factsheets*
Svensson, Charlotte Rosen, *Culture Shock!: Sweden* (Kuperard Ltd, 1997)
Taylor-Wilkie, Doreen, *Insight Guides: Sweden* (APA Publications, 1996)
The Economist, *Pocket World in Figures*, (Profile Books, 2002)
Warme, Lars G. (ed.), *A History of Swedish Literature* (University of Nebraska Press, 1996)

General further reading
Clawson, Elmer, *Activities and Investigations in Economics* (Addison-Wesley, 1994)
The DK Geography of the World. (Dorling Kindersley, 1996)
The Kingfisher History Encyclopedia. (Kingfisher, 1999)
Martell, Hazel Mary, *The Kingfisher Book of the Ancient World* (Kingfisher, 1995)

Student Atlas. New York: Dorling Kindersley, 1998

Further reading about Sweden
Anderson, Margaret J., *Great Minds of Science: Carl Linnaeus: Father of Classification* (Enslow Publishers, 1997)
Annee, Millard, and Claire Craig, *Nature Company Discoveries: Explorers and Traders* (Time Life, 1996)
Carlsson, Bo, *Modern Industrial World: Sweden* (Thompson Learning, 1995)
Lindgren, Astrid, *Pippi Longstocking* (Puffin, 1997)
Morley, Jacqueline, *First Facts: The Vikings* (Peter Bedrick Books, 1996)

Some websites about Sweden
World Travel Guide: Sweden
www.travel-guide.com/data/swe/swe.asp
Statistics Sweden
www.scb.se/indexeng.asp
Embassy of Sweden in London
www.swedish-embassy.org.uk

Index

Acknowledgements

Cover photo credits
Corbis: Paul Almasay

Photo credits
AAKG London: 63, 72, 101; Erich Lessing 64; **Brown Reference Group:** 104 below; **Corbis:** 36, 70, 73; Archivo Iconografico, SA 66; Dave Bartruff 61; Bettmann 112; Jonathan Blair 116; Macduff Everton 20, 22, 23, 47, 58, 77, 83; Michael Gore: Frank Lane Picture Agency 34; Robert van der Hilst 81; Andy Keates: Edifice 107; Charles and Josette Lenars 30; Steve Raymer 87; Hubert Stadler 56; Chase Swift 35; Roger Tidman 78; Francessco Venturi: Kea Publishing Services Ltd 24; **SAAB:** 85; **Swedish Travel and Tourism Council:** Stephan Gabriel 102; Glasriket, Publicum 86; Anders Hanser 103; Kjell-Åke Halldén 105; Mats Jansson 17; Joachim Keitel 96; C. Lundin 26, 40; Hans Nelsäter 115; Partners Reklambyrå 104 top; R. Ryan 45, 75; Turistråd Värmlands 27; Jan Kofod Winther 93; **Tony Stone Images:** Chad Ehlers 38, 94; Robert Everts 91; David Hanson 41, 43; Hideo Kurihara 12; Roine Magnusson 6, 18, 28, 33; Hans Strand 14, 52; **Werner Forman Archive:** Statens Historiska Museet, Stockholm 50, 98; Thjodminjasafn, Reykjavik, Iceland 54.